THE ACTS OF THE APOSTLES

The Acts of the Apostles

TEN LECTURES

by

ARNOLD EHRHARDT

*Late Bishop Fraser Senior Lecturer in
Ecclesiastical History in the
University of Manchester*

MANCHESTER UNIVERSITY PRESS

© MRS E. R. EHRHARDT 1969

Published by the University of Manchester at
THE UNIVERSITY PRESS
316–324 Oxford Road, Manchester M13 9NR

UK standard book number 7190 0382 2

Printed in Great Britain by Butler & Tanner Ltd, Frome and London

Foreword

This is not the first of Arnold Ehrhardt's contributions to the study of the Acts of the Apostles to be published by Manchester University Press: an essay on 'The Construction and Purpose of the Acts of the Apostles' was included in the volume of his collected papers entitled *The Framework of the New Testament Stories*, issued in 1964. That essay in its original form was read to the Lightfoot Society at Durham (that is, to an audience of theological students and teachers) and was later published (1958) in a learned periodical, *Studia Theologica*. The scholars for whom it was intended welcomed it with the appreciation which it merited: it is one of the six treatments of the Lukan writings, for example, which Professor C. K. Barrett singles out for examination in his *Luke the Historian in Recent Study* (1961).

The contents of the present volume were intended for quite a different public: here are ten lectures delivered to members of the 'general public' under the auspices of the Extra-Mural Department of Manchester University. Dr Ehrhardt's immense erudition coexisted happily with a genial friendliness towards ordinary men and women and the capacity for communicating the fruit of his scholarship in terms which they could understand. One feature of the popular character of these lectures is the use of James Moffatt's version for most of the Bible quotations which occur in them; had they been delivered after, and not before, the appearance of the New English Bible, that version would probably have been used.

On the last occasion when I heard Dr Ehrhardt deliver a public lecture (at the Nottingham meeting of the Society of New Testament Studies in 1963), he spoke of his continuing resolution to preserve his 'amateur status' in the New Testament field. His specialist studies lay in the two fields of Roman Law and Early Church History. With the equipment of a student in these fields he found in the New Testament features that usually escape the notice of those who come to it along more conventional paths. He recognized the twofold work of Luke for what it is—the work of a historian in the tradition of Thucydides and Polybius, making judicious use of such sources as were available to him to amplify that part of his narrative for which he could rely on personal knowledge. It is refreshing indeed to find Luke described as 'a glutton for documentary evidence' who 'knew how to use it to the best advantage in his history'. Not that Luke's theological interest and tendency are overlooked in the following pages; but Dr Ehrhardt did not suppose that a man must be an inferior historian because he is an original theologian. Moving back from his studies in Christian history of the second, third and fourth centuries, he regarded Luke's writings as the earliest example of a *genre* for which we have to wait two and a half centuries before we find it manifested again—in the writings of Eusebius. And moving back to Luke's writings from later Christian literature, he found it impossible to regard them as other than a product of the first century, put together by a man who was himself contemporary with at least the later events which he records, and not only contemporary, but an eyewitness of some of them.

Some of the suggestions and interpretations put forward in these lectures are highly individual in character; but even the most unconventional ones demand careful consideration, because of the knowledge and judgment on which they are based. Wherever Dr Ehrhardt disagreed with my own conclusions on various questions arising from the study of Acts, I have always found it profitable to give serious attention to the reasons for his dissent and criticism, and even when I have remained of the same opinion still, my grounds for holding it are firmer because of my study of his counter-arguments.

For a number of years Dr Ehrhardt and I were jointly responsible for the direction of a post-graduate seminar in the University of Manchester concerned with the study of the New Testament and Early Church. The seminar continues its activities, greatly impoverished by the fact that he is no longer with us. Shortly after his death, Mrs Ehrhardt kindly gave permission for his name to be associated with the seminar, and in the name of the Ehrhardt Seminar as well as on my own behalf it is a pleasure to welcome the publication of these lectures and to commend them to a wider public than heard them when they were given in spoken form.

F. F. BRUCE

Contents

1 Time, tradition and canonization of the Book of Acts

Amongst the various books of the New Testament the 'Acts of the Apostles' constitutes a special problem, in that the book claims to be a continuation of the Third Gospel. Not only is it addressed to a person called Theophilus, a name also found in Luke 1:3, but its address also explicitly refers to a Gospel addressed by the same writer to the same Theophilus on an earlier occasion (Acts 1:1 f.):

In my former volume, Theophilus, I treated all that Jesus began by doing and teaching down to the day when, after issuing his orders by the holy Spirit, He was taken up to heaven.

Therefore, since the only Gospel extant which mentions the Ascension is the Third Gospel, there can be no reasonable doubt that the author of Acts claimed to be the author of the Third Gospel also. He was at any rate conversant with the beginning as well as the ending of that Gospel.

It can also be stated that stylistically the Third Gospel and the Book of Acts correspond so closely to each other, that we can without reserve ascribe the two books to the same writer. This is a very important statement. For it was not unusual in the time of the Greeks and Romans to complete the work of any famous author 'in his name' only. The last book of Caesar's *Gallic War*, for instance, was written by Aulus Hirtius, one of his generals, and added to the defective work of his great leader, and there are numerous other instances. For this reason researches into stylistic peculiarities are a necessity, and these have yielded the definite result that the author of the Third Gospel and the author of Acts are one and the same person. They have, moreover, given us a fair insight into the sources used by the author, especially that he has used Aramaic sources up to the fifteenth chapter of Acts, but probably not for the later chapters.

This common author of the two books of the Third Gospel and of Acts is commonly known as St Luke. In the manuscripts of the Gospels the heading 'According to Luke' is always found for the Third Gospel. Nor has this Gospel ever gone under any other name in the references

The Acts of the Apostles

to it in the early Fathers of the Church. This fact may be felt to give us a fair start for the dating of the two books; but as a matter of fact puts us in a serious quandary. For even if we discard, as I feel we must, the reference to St Luke in II Tim. 4:11, we have two genuine references—to St Luke, the 'beloved physician', in Col. 4:14, and just the name in Phm. 24—which show that he was a well-known follower of St Paul. On the other hand, not only is the theology of Acts rather different from that of St Paul, not only is the account of the discord between St Paul and the Church at Jerusalem described in a very different vein in Acts 12–15 from the way in which St Paul himself has recorded it, especially in Galatians, but there are also various hints in the Third Gospel as well as in Acts, which indicate that both these books were written only after the fall of Jerusalem in A.D. 70, and perhaps even a considerable time after it.

As we are here dealing with Acts, I may perhaps point to the most troublesome instance in that book. In the speech of Gamaliel (Acts 5:36 f.) we read:

In days gone by Theudas started up, claiming to be a person of importance; a number of men, about four hundred of them, rallied to him, but he was slain, and all his followers were dispersed and wiped out. After him Judas the Galilean started up, at the time of the census, and got people to desert to him; but he perished too, and all his followers were scattered.

This statement, we would state, is first of all historically wrong, for Judas the Galilean was in time not after but long before Theudas. The rise of Judas was *c*. A.D. 6, whereas that of Theudas was *c*. A.D. 44. This date shows secondly that it had not yet happened at the time when Gamaliel was supposed to have made his speech, *c*. A.D. 34. Both these mistakes, however, would not yet exclude the possibility of a follower of St Paul's being the author of Acts. What makes it difficult to accept such an assumption is the fact that the sequence of Theudas first and Judas second also occurs in the last book of Josephus's *Antiquities of the Jews* (xx. 5. 1 f.). Josephus, however, started on his literary career only after the fall of Jerusalem, and he has stated himself that he did not complete the last book of the *Antiquities* before A.D. 93/4 (*Ant.* xx. 11 *fin.*). If, therefore, it is assumed that St Luke must have read Josephus, before he composed the speech of Gamaliel, the Book of Acts cannot have been written before ± A.D. 100, and that would exclude the identification of its author with 'Luke the beloved physician'.

Many scholars have drawn this conclusion; but we cannot say that

2

we are satisfied with it. There is first a hint at knowledge of Acts in I Clement which, however, in itself is too faint to disprove the theory. It seems to us, all the same, that such a late date for the conception of Acts fails to explain the excellence of the report in the second part of the book, which is commonly referred to as the 'we-report'. For there the author records the experiences of St Paul and his team in the first person plural, as if he himself had been a member of the team. Neither can such a late date explain the abrupt ending of the book. For it is at least very difficult to imagine that an impostor should have made up the earlier part of his story, but should have hesitated at producing an account of St Paul's adventures at Rome, even if he knew nothing about them. It is certain that the mind of the early second-century Church, which produced a great number of apocryphal Acts of various Apostles, did not work in this way. It also suggested by an early third-century source, the so-called Muratorian fragment,[1] that St Paul was set free at Rome and went to Spain, a suggestion rather supported by than derived from Rom. 15:24, 28; there are furthermore persistent rumours that St Paul worked for a time in Illyria. In short, his history was by no means closed at the time when the Book of Acts finishes.

Under these circumstances there are three possibilities for arriving at a more satisfactory date for Acts. The first is that we should regard the similarity with Josephus in Acts 5:37, 38 as a mere coincidence. However, the similarity between the two sources is so close that there is little probability in this assumption. Theoretically the possibility cannot be excluded, but if we wish to be true to the principles of historical method, we have to discard it. For if we deviate from those principles in one single instance, we abandon the basis of our whole Christian faith, that the Son of God was made man in history, not according to any pious dreams and fancies of some enthusiasts. That leaves us with the choice between a theory of 'sources of Acts' and 'sources' of Josephus. For it can either be assumed that the author of Acts drew on materials for—amongst other things—the 'we-report', or that Josephus copied the passage quoted by us from an earlier book, which had also been accessible to St Luke.

The fact that St Luke used earlier sources for part of his narrative is, as we have already stated, beyond doubt; and for this reason most New Testament scholars assume that that is all that is needed to overcome our difficulty. They would maintain that Acts received its final form only $\pm$A.D. 100, but that it embodied material of an earlier age, worked over

[1] Cf. A. Ehrhardt, *The Framework of the New Testament Stories* (Manchester, 1964), pp. 11 ff.

by the man who wrote the preface and—so we are led to believe—pieces like the speech of Gamaliel. Unfortunately this theory does not hold good, because it has been shown that the speeches in Acts follow a similar pattern, stylistically as well as materially, so that the amount of matter produced by the supposed writer of A.D. 100 would be so great as to make the abrupt ending of the book once more inexplicable. Consequently we must assume that St Luke had before him a written account of Gamaliel's addresses upon which he drew, as Josephus did afterwards.

Such being the case, we are free to date Acts at any time between A.D. 75 and A.D. 90, the latest date at which we can reasonably assume that a man might have been active, who as an adult had accompanied St Paul on his journey into Macedonia in A.D. 52, i.e. was born $\pm$A.D. 20. Acts cannot have been written before the fall of Jerusalem, because the Third Gospel cannot have been written before that date, and the Third Gospel is earlier than Acts. However, Acts cannot have been written after A.D. 90, because the case for a member of St Paul's team having written the 'we-report' is too strong. Furthermore it must have been written some time after St Paul's death, for the apostle might have frowned at various things which he is supposed to have said in Acts; but its author, St Luke, did not venture to go beyond the entries in his diaries, for reasons which at the moment we shall leave undiscussed, but which I hope will prove sufficient. A date of $\pm$A.D. 80 seems to us the most reasonable assumption.

II

In Cambridge University Library there lies one of the most puzzling documents for the whole history of Christianity, a manuscript codex of the sixth century A.D., containing the Gospels and Acts in Greek and Latin. The Latin is not a translation of this Greek text, but has its own important place in the realm of biblical criticism.[1] It is, however, the Greek text of this so-called Codex Bezae (named after its first historically known owner, the Swiss reformer Beza) which confronts us with an almost insoluble puzzle. In order to understand this we must enter a little upon the whole matter of the texual criticism of the New Testament.

Let it be sufficient to point out first that the great universal religions which stem from the Near East—Christianity, Judaism and Islam—are

[1] The Greek text of this manuscript is conventionally referred to by the letter 'D'; the Latin text by 'd'.

book religions in a way in which other universal religions, like Buddhism, and most national and primitive religions, are not. Divine service in the Christian Church, the Jewish Synagogue or Islam without a 'reading' is an impossibility. Thus an enormous number of copies of the sacred books was required, and is still required by the Church. Before the invention of the printing press all these copies had to be produced by hand. The language of the New Testament, however, was very similar to the everyday Greek speech of the times and regions in which it arose. Consequently the task of copying the New Testament was made very difficult to contemporaries, because the book appeared to them in no special festal guise, but in everyday attire, so that a word might easily be replaced by a synonym, the article left out or added, even the tenses changed, without any appreciable change in the meaning as far as the copyists themselves were concerned. These variants are a constant mortification to the conscientious New Testament scholar, but the process of weeding them out is in constant progress; and modern translations, like Moffatt's, which we are using, show that the intelligibility of the New Testament is increased by these untiring efforts.

Comparatively speaking, the critic's task becomes easier when he is faced with textual variants intended to change the meaning of the text. For where there were doctrinal reasons for such a change—and what other reason can there be behind such a change of meaning?—it is often possible to point to tendencies within or heresies outside the Catholic Church, which are likely to have occasioned these differences. In 'D', the Greek text of Codex Bezae, however, the changes which occur seem to amount to a re-edition of Acts in an appreciably different tenor. The balance between St Paul and the Church at Jerusalem in the canonical Acts (which we read in our common versions), so carefully established by its author, is very subtly changed in favour of the Jerusalem Church in 'D'. St Paul is firmly put in subjection to the decisions as well as to the organization of the mother Church.

If there existed no more than the witness of this sixth-century manuscript, and a few others of a still later date, it need not disturb us unduly. We would have to face the question, of course, why Christians at the time of the conquest of Italy by the Goths and of Gaul by the Franks should have interfered so much with the text of the Acts of the Apostles; and we might have tried wrongly to answer this question with the help of contemporary Church history. However, the variants of 'D' may be found all over the christianized world. They appear in certain Syriac translations of the New Testament, originating from Antioch and the regions further East, as well as in a group of Coptic translations from Egypt. In the far North-East they occur in Armenian witnesses, but also in Latin translations in the West. Most disquieting of all these circumstances is the fact that they play their part also in the quotations from the New Testament in the early Church Fathers. That compels us to conclude that they, like most other variants in the New Testament, go back to the second century. A very learned German scholar, Friedrich Blass, even devoted his whole commentary on Acts to the attempted proof that St Luke himself produced two editions of Acts, of which that in 'D' is the later and therefore the valid one.[1]

F. Blass's proof has failed, but the discrepancies between the canonical recension of Acts and that in 'D' shed light upon discussions within the Church of the second century of which little is known otherwise. It is the division between the Judaizers and the Paulinists within the Catholic Church. It appears that the region which was most in favour of Pauline theology, Asia Minor, produced a whole literature of Acts of various Apostles, and that Antioch, where the judaizing tendencies were strongest, retorted with the pseudo-Clementine literature, because even the Acts in its 'D' form did not provide a sufficiently strong counterblast. For there can be no doubt that there is a fairly strong anti-Jewish strain underlying Acts, with which the Judaizers within the Catholic Church could not possibly concur, even if it intended to show that the Christian Church was in fact the 'Israel of God', and subordinated St Paul to St Peter, as Alfred Loisy has suggested.[2]

If it is possible to test the importance of Acts for the early Church by these indirect means, it appears that direct testimonies for the use of Acts by the Church of the first half of the second century are very scarce. This is most surprising in the case of the arch-heretic Marcion. We know that he took the Third Gospel (*c.* A.D. 135) for the Gospel of the Marcionite Church; but there is no evidence that he ever used Acts. How are we to explain this? Two things will come to mind at once: one, that in spite of St Luke's different intentions the Third Gospel and Acts were not treated by the early Church as the two parts of one book, but as two separate works, so that it was possible to accept the one and to neglect the other; the second, that we have to make up our minds as to whether Marcion rejected or simply ignored Acts, and that on very scanty

[1] F. Blass, *Acta Apostolorum sive Lucas ad Theophilum liber alter* (Göttingen, 1895); cf. his *Acta Apostolorum secundum formam quae videtur Romanam* (Leipzig, 1896).

[2] A. Loisy, *The Origins of the New Testament*, E.T. (London, 1950), pp. 179 ff.; cf. his *Les Actes des Apôtres* (Paris, 1920).

evidence indeed. This latter question is of immediate importance for us because of the problem of the place of origin of Acts, which we have not discussed so far. If Acts was used in the Church at Rome in the time of Marcion, we must assume that he rejected it, for his final separation from the Catholic Church took place at Rome, and his 'Gospel' and his 'Apostle'—a selection from the Pauline Epistles—upon which he founded his separatist Church, were based upon New Testament writings which were current in the Church at Rome during his stay there. If he simply ignored Acts, there is a good chance that the book was not yet in general use at Rome, and further that it is not likely to have originated from Rome.

Once more the evidence is ambiguous. On the one hand, there is nothing in the teaching of Marcion suggesting that he took exception to the theological attitude of Acts. Although there is a marked difference between St Luke's and St Paul's theology, and although Marcion was an admirer of St Paul, that difference does not concern the particular teaching of Marcion; and it may even be held that the evidence about St Paul's life and work, as contained in Acts, would have been of great value to a Church so avowedly Pauline as the Marcionite Church. On the other hand, there are slight traces of a knowledge of Acts in the Church at Rome as early as the end of the first century in I Clement, too slight, as we have seen, even to make this testimony of any great value for the dating of the book. Similar traces may be found in Justin Martyr and Tatian, two Fathers who are, however, also dependent on traditions other than the Roman tradition. This would go for very little indeed, if non-Roman evidence were any more substantial. But only from the Church at Smyrna, from the Epistle and the Martyrdom of Polycarp, can we derive any indications that the Acts were read at all in the Catholic Church in the first half of the second century. If it were not for the evidence provided by the contrast between the two versions of Acts in the two different groups of manuscripts, and the rise of a whole literature of apocryphal Acts of the various Apostles, we would know precious little of the influence of Acts upon early Christianity right up to the end of the second century. As it is, we can posit a rivalry between the two great provinces of the Church in the East in this matter, the Church of Asia Minor, centred round Ephesus and Smyrna, on the one hand, and the Church of Syria, centred round Antioch, on the other. We can state with some conviction that early traditions of the Church, by which St Luke was made a native of Antioch, fit in with the fact that his Acts of the Apostles seems to have appealed strongly to Christians living in those parts of the Roman Empire: not perhaps by the letter, but by that spirit which gave to the apostles a paramount importance in the Church of the second century such as they had scarcely enjoyed in the first.

III

How then did the Acts of the Apostles become part of the New Testament of the Catholic Church? With this question we have described what we mean by the 'canonization' of Acts. To answer this question we must once more take into account the whole of the New Testament. For it has to be said that the process of canonization was a gradual one, and that the canonization of Acts was not the first step taken by the Church in the selection of books qualifying as Holy Scripture. From its beginning the Church had a Bible, the Old Testament of the Jews, which Catholic Christians claimed as the rightful property of the Christian Church, rather than of the Jewish Synagogue. Both these bodies found it necessary in the course of the first two centuries to add of their own experiences to that old collection of Holy Scriptures; but whereas the Synagogue did not close the evolution of sacred teaching, but preserved the decisions of many generations of Rabbis in its Mishnah, the Church at once limited the eligibility of writings for inclusion in its New Testament canon to those produced by men of its apostolic age, if not to the apostles themselves. The need for such a limitation came from the fact that in the Church, right down to the middle of the second century, prophecy, which the Synagogue abhorred, was encouraged. This called for 'proving the spirits' in the Church, and the earliest advice regarding this procedure may be found in I John 4:1 f. However, the method proposed there:

You can recognize the Spirit of God by this: every spirit which confesses Jesus as the Christ incarnate comes from God; and any spirit which does not confess Jesus incarnate does not come from God—

this method, we say, was in need of implementation.

For this purpose the genuine writings of apostles and apostolic men were required, for the schisms and heresies amongst the early Christians were innumerable. Such a state of affairs was also to be expected, since every Christian was furnished with the gift of the Spirit through baptism. Naturally two particular groups of writings were scrutinized first for their suitability to serve as Holy Scripture, far in advance of all others: the Gospels, as witnessing to the first advent of the Lord in humility, and the Apocalypses, as witnessing to His expected second coming in glory. Of the former all but four were rejected, and of the latter all but one.

This then was the first step in the canonization of the New Testament writings. The next was the establishment of these very apostles and apostolic men as true witnesses to Jesus as the Christ incarnate by their own inspired utterances. It was in the course of this second examination that the book of Acts was brought under close scrutiny by the Church.

Once more our best evidence for these events is internal evidence. The title of our book, 'The Acts of the Apostles', is obviously a later addition. First of all, it does not fit the contents of our book, which only records some period of the life of St Peter and St Paul, and gives details of no more than two other apostles, St James and St John; but which, on the other hand, introduces a whole number of characters, St Stephen and St Philip, St James of Jerusalem and St Barnabas and many others, who at best were only just mentioned once in the Gospel, or played no part in it at all. Just as it was with most other literary productions of that period, the second book of St Luke's work received no separate title from its author.

However, the name under which our book is known now was not a neutral one, but contained a programme. 'The Acts of the Apostles' does not just mean the records of the apostles, but the 'achievements', even the miraculous achievements of the apostles, the way in which they proved themselves to be true apostles of Jesus Christ. If, therefore, the title is only partly borne out by the contents of the book, it has nevertheless a good Lukan ring, for it seems to be suggested by Luke 10:19:

I have indeed given you the power of treading on serpents and scorpions and of trampling down all the power of the Enemy; nothing shall injure you.

Thus the title of the book may explicitly make a claim which, in view of St Paul's encounter with the viper (Acts 28:3 f.) and of all the other miracles performed by St Peter and St Paul in his book, the author might have made himself. All the same the title is also the result of that craving for apostolicity amongst Christians of the second century, at a time when apostolic and canonical became almost synonyms.

The second piece of evidence for the canonization of Acts is circumstantial evidence. In the course of the second century Asia Minor produced a group of five books of apocryphal Acts, the so-called Acts of Leucius, comprising the adventures of St Peter, St Paul, St John, St

B

Thomas and St Andrew. They were widely read both in Catholic and gnostic circles. A reference from Catholic circles in Egypt may still be found in Origen, the great Father of the first half of the third century, whereas Tertullian, his somewhat earlier African contemporary, hints at some catastrophe which befell their author, apparently when an enquiry into their apostolic origin was made. Tertullian says that the author was a priest of the Catholic Church in Asia. This in itself suggests that by the middle of the second century the process of canonization of this type of literature was already set in motion in Asia; and this suggestion is reinforced by the fact, established by M. R. James,[1] that the five books of Leucius did indeed become part of the holy scriptures of the Manichees.

It has been necessary to draw out this background in order to make us understand the fact that our book of Acts just emerges as canonical, without further discussion, in Catholic Fathers and documents originating from the end of the second century A.D. For the first direct witness for the canonicity of Acts is Irenaeus, bishop of Lyons ±A.D. 180, a native of Smyrna in Asia. At the same time the bishop of Antioch, also named Theophilus, added his witness to the canonicity of Acts. On the other hand, Clement of Alexandria, who wrote his works also during the last two decades of the second century, treated St Luke's book of Acts with respect as a reliable witness to conditions in the apostolic period, but did not yet regard the book as Holy Scripture. Egypt had not then, so it appears, made up its mind even with regard to the relative importance of the canonical Gospels and their apocryphal counterparts which there, more than elsewhere, circulated widely; and was thus not ready for the canonization of Acts.

It is only from the beginning of the third century that we have the earliest direct witness to the canonicity of Acts originating from the Church at Rome, the Muratorian fragment, a document to which we have referred already. This is the fragment of a catalogue of those books which are, or are not, to be read in Church, as constituting the New Testament of that particular Church. Its witness is especially valuable because it attempts to give reasons for their acceptance by the Church. This is what it has to say about Acts:

But the Acts of all the Apostles are written in one book. Luke dedicates it, 'my best Theophilus', because of everything taking place in his presence. Similarly

---

[1] M. R. James, *Apocrypha Anecdota* i, ii = *Texts and Studies* ii. 3, v, 1 (Cambridge, 1893, 1897); *The Apocryphal New Testament* (Oxford, 1924), pp. xx f., 228 ff.

also he separately mentions clearly the passion of Peter and also the journey of Paul from Rome to Spain.[1]

It seems probable that the writer confused Luke and Leucius, for the second sentence refers clearly to the apocryphal Acts of St Peter by Leucius, and thus illustrates how difficult it was even then to separate the pure gold from the dross. At the same time, however, Tertullian had already used Acts in his violent attack upon Marcion, who claimed that St Paul by his conflict with St Peter at Antioch, and by his refusal 'to yield for a single instant to their claims' (Gal. 2:5), had proved himself to be the only true apostle of Jesus Christ. Acts served Tertullian in this attack of his as full proof of the complete harmony between the two apostles.

This, however, is already entering upon the substance of Acts, rather than upon the early external history of the book. Our task in this first lecture has been achieved when we have made it clear that the book is a very early witness to the first years of the Christian Church; that we have every reason to assume that it has now come into our hands substantially intact, in spite of at least one most determined attack upon the integrity of its text; that it is by no means just a historical narrative of more or less memorable events, but rather one of the most controversial treatises in the New Testament; and finally that from the beginning of the third century the whole Catholic Church has without interruption acknowledged that the book of Acts shows that spiritual power by which the books of the New Testament are distinguished from secular or even other Christian, devotional writings.

[1] Col. 1, 1. 34. See A. Ehrhardt, *The Framework of the New Testament Stories* (Manchester, 1964), p. 18.

2 St Peter and the Twelve

The Acts of the Apostles is one of the most interesting documents of Graeco-Roman times. One of the greatest historians of our time, the German Eduard Meyer, perhaps the most universal mind amongst historians of antiquity at the beginning of our century, with whom only the Russian Michael Rostovtzeff can be compared, has rightly placed Acts in the same rank with Thucydides, Polybius, Tacitus and Eusebius, i.e. with those historians of antiquity who attempted to give a critical account of the great events of their own time in the light of their reasoned as well as reasonable historical judgment.[1] Such then is the historian's approach. However, our exegesis has to be more comprehensive still. It would be fatal for the theologian to neglect the historical approach, but it is equally fatal to give too little consideration to the fact that St Luke claimed to be the historian of events of more than human significance. His book is not meant to be just a history of the Primitive Church but, as we have seen, makes the claim of describing 'the acts', the divinely guided actions, of the apostles. Admittedly, the title is a later addition, but it is really deficient only in one respect. It should read 'The Acts of the Apostles of Jesus the Christ'.

St Luke, so it appears to us, has made it very evident, not only by the first verses of Acts, but by the whole opening of the book, that it was his intention to continue the story of Jesus Christ in his second book. There is a clear parallelism between the opening of the Gospel and the opening of Acts. The Third Gospel begins with a prehistoric, 'mythological' account of the annunciation and the birth of Jesus as well as of His forerunner John the Baptist. In exactly the same way the book of Acts begins with the prehistoric, 'mythological' account of the ascension. What we mean by these two terms is this: the Gospel narrative of St Luke nowhere makes explicit reference to the circumstances of Jesus's nativity, which is described with angels and shepherds and all the paraphernalia of a 'sacred story' of ancient mythology. However, if the miraculous birth-story were forgotten, the working up of the Third

[1] E. Meyer, *Ursprung und Anfänge des Christentums* i (Berlin, 1921), pp. 2 f.

Gospel to its resurrection-reports would make no sense. Equally Acts nowhere mentions the ascension; but whilst the conclusion that the Third Gospel needs the Christmas story for its master-key is frequently drawn, the report on the ascension has not yet been granted the same distinction, which, however, it deserves.

This follows from the fact that the parallelism between the Third Gospel and Acts is continued. We have the intermediate period with the story of the twelve-year-old Jesus in the Gospel, and we have the story of the election of St Matthias to the chair of Judas in Acts. He too vanishes from the scene for ever after. Finally we have the story of the Holy Spirit descending upon Jesus in St John's baptism, which introduces the record of His ministry; and we have the miracle of Pentecost in Acts, which introduces the record of His Church. Possibly a parallel could also be drawn between Jesus's inaugural sermon at Nazareth and St Peter's at Pentecost. Let me add at once that St Luke is far too good a writer and too honest an historian to labour this parallelism; but the structural similarity is close enough to deserve our careful attention. That means that we must not forget that St Luke put Jesus Christ Himself in the centre not only of his Gospel, but also of Acts.

II

Having stated this, we must follow the angel's advice not to 'stand looking up to heaven', but follow the Eleven to Jerusalem. Like them we are beset by numerous questions. They were 'men of Galilee'; what would be their abode in Jerusalem? They were the witnesses of Christ's ascension; but there were a considerable number of further witnesses to His resurrection, and what was their mutual relationship in His Church to be? Finally, they were the spiritual brothers and friends of Jesus, but how was this to be brought into line with those who claimed a blood-relationship with Jesus? All these questions were put at once when they arrived in Jerusalem, where they met with 'the women, with Mary the mother of Jesus and with his brothers' (Acts 1:14), and with the 'crowd of about a hundred and twenty persons all together'. For there are clearly these three different groups, the Eleven with 'the women' ('their wives'?), the mother and brothers of Jesus, and 'the crowd'.

It is also evident that St Peter tackled the problem at once in his own way. For him it was the problem of preparing for the second advent of

Christ, which the angel of the ascension had predicted. His commission to do so is to be found in Luke 22:30:

I assign you the right of eating and drinking at my table in my Realm and of sitting on thrones to rule the twelve tribes of Israel.

Not only the question put in Acts 1:6, 'Lord, is this the time you are going to restore the Realm to Israel?' but still more so the elevation of St Matthias to the chair vacated by the defection of Judas Iscariot shows that the Twelve almost hourly expected the return of Jesus in his glory. Their representative was St Peter, and it seems a fair statement if we ascribe to him and to the other eleven a theology as well as a policy with a clear eschatological direction.

For the time being this eschatological attitude carried the day. For the miracle of Pentecost was a truly eschatological event. It has become the fashion in modern time to stress that this miracle was the divine reversal of the confusion of tongues which caused the abandonment of the tower of Babel. Neither do we deny the validity of this exegesis. However, this exegesis does not account for the most pronounced feature of Pentecost, the 'tongues like flames distributing themselves, one resting on the head of each'. As far as we know there is no Old Testament reference to this; and yet we feel that such a reference is required. Only as an hypothesis we venture to suggest that the Midrash to Deut. 5:22 f., mentioned by Philo, which maintained that the Law of Sinai was spread in all languages and amongst all nations, made reference to Deut. 5:24: 'we have heard his voice out of the flames, we have seen today how a man can live after God has spoken to him'. We would therefore suggest that St Peter and the Twelve, coming from the mount of the ascension, are represented here in the part of Moses, proposing the New Covenant of the 'last days', when the power of the Spirit was to be given to the children of Israel.

Such is also the gist of St Peter's sermon which, however, for lack of time, we cannot analyse in detail. We have to limit our remarks to two necessary observations. The first concerns the curious introduction, 'they are brim-full of new wine' (Acts 2:13), and St Peter's reply. Modern commentators have taken this quite literally, although the time for the new wine was not yet at hand. This recognition gives to the accusation as well as to the defence of St Peter (Acts 2:14), 'Why, it is only nine,' more weight than the customary, and doubtful, reference to the Talmudic prescript that the pious Jew should fast before morning prayer (at 9 a.m.). For there is no reference to morning prayer in Acts 2.

We would rather refer to allegorical language like that in Luke 5:37, 'no one pours fresh wine into old wineskins'. This observation also removes, we feel, the unfortunate association of after-dinner speech.

Our second observation is the curious discrepancy between the promise in Joel 2:28, 'then will I pour out my spirit upon all flesh' (Moffatt omits in his Old Testament translation Heb. *bāśār*, 'flesh'—why?), and the answer given by Peter to the repentant Jews (Acts 2:39). 'For the promise is meant for you and for your children and for all who are far off, for anyone whom the Lord our God may call to himself.' First of all, this is not a quotation, as the italics in Moffatt may suggest. The reference is to Is. 57:19 (LXX),[1] 'peace upon peace to those who are afar and to those who are near', and to the end of Joel 2:32 (not previously quoted in St Peter's sermon), 'and blessed are they whom the Lord calls to Himself in Jerusalem and on mount Sion'. Thus it is a conflation rather than a quotation. Secondly, and this is important, Joel's prophecy was to 'all flesh', and that was the technical term which the Jews employed for 'all mankind'; but that from Isaiah is ambiguous; it may only refer to the Jews of the dispersion. St Peter evidently chose the second alternative.

This is indeed a highly significant conclusion. For it shows that the first public statement of St Peter's strictly followed the line laid down by the question of the Twelve (Acts 1:6), 'Lord is this the time you are going to restore the Realm to Israel?' It was the tradition of the Jews that Jerusalem and Mount Zion would be of universal importance to all mankind at some future time, when the end would come; but the idea was rather that it would be through the conversion and concentration of all Israel throughout the world, that the Gentiles would be brought into the fold. At any rate, for the time being the preaching of the Gospel was for the Jews. That brings to mind Matt. 10:5 f., 'do not go among the Gentiles, and do not enter a Samaritan town; rather make your way to the lost sheep of Israel', the advice of Jesus at the sending out of the Twelve. This advice as you may know, is peculiar to Matthew; neither Luke nor Mark has it, and Matthew, as we believe, is the latest of the Synoptic Gospels. We have to leave it at that for the time being, and will return to it when we discuss the confirmation of the Samaritans by St Peter and St John, and the conversion of Cornelius the centurion. At the moment it is essential to stress only the importance of the temple on Mount Zion for this assumedly earliest type of Christian evangelization.

---

[1] LXX is the conventional abbreviation for the 'Septuagint', the pre-Christian Greek translation of the Old Testament.

III

For the next great question in the career of St Peter was exactly this, to whom the temple on Mount Zion should belong.

The question may sound silly to the superficial reader: the temple had been rebuilt by Herod the Great and his successors, and had been dedicated to the service of Yahweh, the God of Israel. However, this was neither sufficient to make it a temple of Yahweh, nor even to justify the holding of services for Yahweh in that temple. We must remember that Herod had been an Edomite, not a Jew; and there was certainly no evidence from the Old Testament that Yahweh would accept a temple dedicated to him by an Edomite. Long after the fall of Jerusalem we find the Rabbis still discussing the question whether any present given to Yahweh by a Gentile should be accepted by the priests of his temple. Moreover, the validity of the priestly office of these priests ministering in the Herodian temple was by no means beyond question. When the Jews had returned from the Babylonian exile, they had been given the clear advice by the prophets of Yahweh, especially Haggai and Zechariah, that his temple should be rebuilt. His high priest, Joshua, had come home with them, and there could then be no doubt that he was entrusted with the resumption of the temple services, as they had been performed under the Davidic kingdom. Even a scion of the house of David, Zerubbabel, had accompanied the returning Jews. What disaster befell him is unknown. Ezra and Nehemiah, who completed the reconstitution of Jerusalem and Judaism, only mention his name. The Davidic kingdom was not restored.

Even so the second temple had God's blessing until, in the days of the Maccabees, 'the abomination of desolation' had taken possession of it, and that by the very treason of a high priest, Menelaus, of the line of Joshua, the line indicated by the prophets.[1] A new line of high priests had therefore to be inaugurated, when finally the Maccabees had recaptured Jerusalem and Mount Zion from the hellenized Syrians. However, there was then no confirmation of this step by an acknowledged prophet of Yahweh. Thus the first book of Maccabees records (14:41):

that the Jews and the priests were well pleased that Simon should be their leader and high priest for ever, until there should arise a faithful prophet.

---

[1] So Josephus, *Antiquities* xii.5.1; according to II Maccabees 4:23 (together with 3:4), Menelaus was an interloper from quite another line.

In other words, the high priesthood of the Maccabean house was only on approval. However, even this conditional high priesthood had come to an end. The Roman Pompey had defiled the temple of Yahweh again in 63 B.C., and now the new house was built by an Edomite and the high priests were appointed by the Roman government. Their title to form the key-stone for the whole worship of the most high God was of the shakiest.

Such was the background for the miracle and the sermon at the Beautiful Gate. The political threat in St Peter's quotation in Acts 3:22 f. of the prophecy from Deut. 18:15, 19, should have been noticed by the commentators who, however, seem singularly blind to the significance of the localization of the miracle. Yet the quotation is, as F. F. Bruce has correctly pointed out,[1] not from the LXX, and at the same time a conflation of two separate verses from Deut. 18, followed by a still more inaccurate quotation from Lev. 23:29, as the following comparison will show:

Acts 3:23	*Lev. 23:29*
Any soul that will not listen to this prophet shall be exterminated from the people.	Whoever will not abstain and fast on that day shall be outlawed from his kinsfolk.

Is it so easy to assume that St Luke, who knew his LXX very well, should have drawn on a collection of Christian 'testimonies' at such a critical juncture? We feel certain that the answer must be in the negative, and that St Peter here was made to use Jewish material in connection with the hope for a Messianic high priest, of which we know something from the recently discovered as well as from earlier Jewish sectarian writings, but also from Josephus.

It is from this basis that we have to judge the action of the priests and Sadducees who took this quotation for their cue to call the commander of the temple guard to have St Peter and St John arrested. The mention of the Sadducees may, of course, have been caused by their general opposition to the doctrine of the resurrection; but it was the whole Messianic diction of the sermon, endangering the only seemingly legal order in Jerusalem, to which they objected.

Let me say just one word about the disappearance of the struggle between the Christians and the Jewish sects in Acts. It is surprising that St Luke who, in his Gospel, has recorded the antagonism between Jesus and the Pharisees just as much as the other Gospel writers, does not mention

[1] *The Acts of the Apostles* (London, 1952), p. 113.

this conflict in Acts any more. Two possible explanations are at hand, the one that a considerable number of Pharisees were received into the Church (in favour of this one may quote Acts 15:5, where it is expressly stated that St Paul's opponents at the so-called council of the apostles were Christians 'who belonged to the Pharisaic party'); the other that it was from loyalty to St Paul himself. Neither of these two explanations is really satisfactory; but we can state from the evidence in Acts with some confidence, that Jesus's conflicts with the Pharisees belong to reports of a pre-Lukan origin.

St Peter and St John, being described in Acts 4:13 as 'uncultured persons and mere outsiders', were not 'scribes' and probably not Pharisees, but the expression does not mean that they were illiterate. At the same time there is here a hint to the explanation of a problem which has puzzled commentators, how it was that the Sanhedrin was 'astonished' at St Peter's 'freedom of speech', and 'could not say anything' (Acts 4:13, 14). It is alleged that the Jewish authorities must have been aware of their successes in evangelizing the masses and therefore must have been prepared for their readiness to answer. The whole scene of St Peter and St John before the Sanhedrin has therefore been called in question. The criticism may be just; but the reason given is slight. All that we can say is that St Luke made this scene into his first great instance of the fulfilment of Christ's promise (Luke 12:11, 12):

When they bring you before synagogues and the magistrates and authorities, do not trouble yourselves about how to defend yourselves or what to say, for the holy Spirit will teach you at that hour what you should say.

That is proved by the repetition of the Greek word *parrhēsia*, which Moffatt has translated as 'outspoken' in Acts 4:13, in the prayer in Acts 4:29:

So now, O Lord, consider the threats of these men, and grant that thy servants may *with all parrhēsia* (Moffatt: perfectly fearless) speak thy word.

There can, of course, be no doubt that the scene of the two apostles before the Sanhedrin is stylized. In fact it is a well known pattern which St Luke has used in this case—the pattern which is also to be found in both the Christian Acts and the so-called Acts of Martyrs. It is a pattern which comes from Jewish literature, as may be seen, for example, from IV Macc. 6:11: 'even by his own torturers was Eleazar admired because of his courage'. This pattern does not, however, prove either the historicity or otherwise of the events described in Acts 3 and 4. Is there any chance of coming to such a conclusion? We have already noticed the discrepancy between the testimonies in Acts 3:22 f. and the LXX, and we take this as a sign for the pre-Lukan origin of the speech in Acts 3:12 ff. Another point to consider is to be found in 3:21: 'Christ who must be kept in heaven till the period of the great Restoration.' The exegesis of the Church has tended to find in this the promise of a cosmic restoration; but it is doubtful whether that is visualized in the speech. The Old Testament strongly suggests the restoration of Israel only, rather than that of the whole world. Thus we receive the impression that we are faced here with an address of a very early origin going back, perhaps, to one of the apostles.

Most disquieting, on the other hand, are Moffatt's brackets round verse 16, which only just hint at the difficulties encountered in the Greek with regard to the inclusion in the sermon of the healed lame beggar; and there the matter stands: St Luke used a speech from an earlier source to support the historicity of the miracle. He needed the miracle to lend more authority to the teaching of the Twelve in 'Solomon's portico', i.e. within the precincts of the temple. There is, on the other hand, no evidence where his information about the miracle came from.

The teaching in the 'portico of Solomon' should be contrasted with the well-known fact that another Jewish sect, the Essenes, entirely abstained from worship at the temple, whereas the Christians attended it regularly, expecting the true High Priest, Jesus Christ, to return and to set things right. Just as we have later, in Acts 23:6, a witness to the jealousy between Pharisees and Sadducees with regard to the control of the affairs of the temple, we feel that in Acts 3:11 ff. a claim for its Christian control is being made. The peaceful picture of small groups in various corners of the huge outer temple square, which is so frequently drawn, does not agree very well with the general anti-Jewish tendency of Acts, or in particular with the 'ignorance' ascribed to the Jewish rulers (Acts 3:17, in contrast to John 11:51, 'he was high priest that year and his words were a prophecy that Jesus was to die for the nation').

IV

We have to assume that the dismissal of St Peter and St John by the Sanhedrin without punishment established the Twelve, under St Peter's leadership, as something like recognized representatives of the new Christian sect. This is implied by the fact that St Luke now turns to the internal affairs of the Primitive Church, its generally communistic way of life, under the supervision of the apostles. Here we have had to decide whether Acts 2:42–47 and 4:32–37 should be regarded as two separate reports or only as one. Our conclusion has been that the latter is the true answer. For in 4:32 f. there is omitted the highly important and well-attested feature of regular common meals among the members of the mother Church. Adding this to the report at the end of Acts 4, we find in it the description of the life of a Jewish sect—not a 'synagogue'—for which we have ample parallels from Philo and Josephus, from the so-called Zadokite Document, and from the Manual of Discipline, one of the Dead Sea Scrolls. We can also draw a parallel to what we know about the Roman *collegia tenuiorum* (the 'friendly societies' of the Empire) and the fraternities of Greek philosophers. Everywhere there is a board like the Twelve, in charge of affairs, common meals with a religious ritual ennobling its restorative purposes, and a common treasury used for relief purposes. One further Jewish feature deserves to be stressed: the 'young men' who carry away the bodies of Ananias and Sapphira (Acts 5:6, 10) are well-known from Jewish inscriptions, and may well be the fore-runners of the later group of 'neophytes'.

Two events have been quoted by St Luke in order to show that this outwardly *petit-bourgeois* gathering was in fact the Church of Christ and the Church of the Spirit. The one is the exceptional liberality bestowed upon it by St Barnabas (Acts 4:36, 37); the other is the story of Ananias and Sapphira. Regarding the first, a certain contrast is usually felt to exist between Acts 4:32,

Now there was but one heart and one soul among the multitude of the believers; not one of them considered anything his personal property, they shared all they had with one another,

and Acts 4:36, 37:

Thus Joseph, who was surnamed Barnabas . . . by the apostles, a Levite of Cypriote birth, sold a farm belonging to him and brought the money, which he placed before the feet of the apostles.

We have to realize, however, that communism was not a carefully worked out system at the time of the apostles, and was not made a law by the Church. Two aspects of St Luke's report on this communism of the Primitive Church should be kept in mind. The first is the exceedingly low standard of living in the time of the Greeks and Romans. Gustav Dalman conducted a series of extensive enquiries into the social conditions obtaining in Palestine at the time of Jesus,[1] from which it is evident that the poverty prevailing there in those days is almost unimaginable. To find an approximation, delete from modern life cotton and potatoes, and find out what remains. The early Christians clubbed together and thus fared a little better through helping each other. The fact, however, that a real land-owner should have sold his estate and distributed the proceeds, exposing himself to the vagaries and miseries of life without money, was an event to be remembered to this day, over two thousand years.

The second consideration to be made is concerned with the person involved. The person is St Barnabas. We cannot now discuss more than the way in which he made his entry into the first community of Christians. St Luke uses an unusual preposition for that which is translated by Moffatt 'surnamed . . . *by* the apostles'—the Greek *apo*, meaning 'from,' 'of'—and it can be very questionable whether Moffatt's translation is correct. As a matter of fact I believe that it cannot be maintained at all, unless the preposition is exchanged for another, and such an operation is clearly excluded by manuscript evidence. It is much more likely that he is 'Barnabas of the apostles', for the translation given of his name by St Luke is obviously wrong, a 'popular' etymology, as you will find pointed out by Cadbury,[2] and thus there was no reason for the apostles to give him the name by which he is known. This conclusion is of great importance, since we have at least two instances of people buying their way into the Church in early Church history. The one is that of Marcion, the arch-heretic, who made a large donation to the Church at Rome on his arrival there, somewhere around A.D. 135. This sum, as Eusebius records, was refunded to him at his expulsion from the Church. The other is that of Cyprian, the famous martyr bishop of Carthage, in the middle of the third century. His liberality and his wealth secured his election as bishop at a time when he was still a neophyte. We ought to compare these reports on the one hand with the censuring remarks in Jas. 2:2 f., and on the other with the struggle for free sitting accommodation in our own Lancashire churches in the course of the nineteenth century. Then we will see more clearly the ethos behind the sequence of the stories of Barnabas and of Ananias and Sapphira.

Turning to the story of these two, we have to remember that St Luke

[1] G. H. Dalman, *Arbeit und Sitte in Palästina* i–vi (Gütersloh, 1928–39).

[2] H. J. Cadbury, 'Some Semitic Personal Names in Luke–Acts', in *Amicitiae Corolla*, ed. H. G. Wood (London, 1933), pp. 47 f.; cf. *The Book of Acts in History* (New York, 1955), p. 24.

is the evangelist of the poor. His Gospel goes far beyond the others both in the demands made on the rich and the denunciation of money as well as in the blessing of the poor. It is my opinion that St Luke who, as a doctor, belonged to the more affluent classes, was constantly troubled in his conscience as to whether he had any right to suffer less hardship than the poor. Evidently the approach to the question of poverty made in Jas. 2:2 f. and the description of the troubles at the common meals in the Corinthian church in I Cor. 11:17 ff. betray a much more matter-of-fact approach to the social problem than its idealization by St Luke. Thus the story of Ananias and Sapphira is St Luke's test case for the question 'whether a rich man can be saved', title of that famous treatise by Clement of Alexandria. From this point of view, Acts 5:4 is the salient point in the whole story:

When it remained unsold did it not remain your own? And even after the sale, was the money not yours to do as you pleased about it?

This verse is, so to speak, St Luke's own reply to his question, maintaining that earthly riches are not in themselves bad, but that they constitute a very sore temptation to become bad.

If that is the personal approach of St Luke to the question of the right or wrong use of riches, Acts 5:4 contains yet another, more general approach to the whole story of the two earliest defaulters of the Church. It reveals the judicial power of St Peter. Whilst this power was stated in the abstract in Matt. 16:19,

I will give you the keys of the Realm of heaven: Whatever you prohibit on earth will be prohibited in heaven; and whatever you permit on earth will be permitted in heaven,

St Luke has exemplified it in the actual verdict of St Peter upon Ananias and Sapphira. St Peter is here depicted as wielding that power which had been granted to him at Caesarea Philippi, after he had professed that Jesus was the Christ of God. This then is meant, we take it, to give the culmination of St Peter's career at the head of the mother Church.

We have to state, however, that this was no more than a preliminary success. It should be contrasted with evidence coming from St Paul (I Cor. 5:3, 4),

For my part, present with you in spirit, though absent in body, I have already, as in your presence, passed sentence on such an offender as this, by the authority of our Lord Jesus Christ,

which shows that such a judicial power was also claimed by the Apostle of the Gentiles. Finally, in John 20:23, it is 'the disciples', witnesses to Christ's resurrection, to whom the risen Lord says,

If you remit the sins of any, they are remitted; if you retain them, they are retained.

St Peter had yet to pass through much suffering and deep humiliation to become what Jesus had promised he would be, the 'rock on which I will build my Church'; but these experiences belong to a period which can no more be described by the title of 'St Peter and the Twelve'.

3　St Stephen and the other Six

We have made a rather rapid progress through the first four and a half chapters of Acts in order to follow the steep ascent of St Peter and the Twelve to that point where the mother Church at Jerusalem is fully established, and we have stopped rather at the end of the story of Ananias and Sapphira than at the end of chapter 5, because we feel that Acts 5:12,

Now they all without exception met in the portico of Solomon,

makes reference to Acts 3:11:

all the people rushed awestruck to them in what was called Solomon's portico.

This suggests to us that there are here two seams discoverable. Therefore the sermon of St Peter, which has already appeared as an alien element, the first arrest of St Peter and St John, their defence before the Sanhedrin and preliminary dismissal, and finally the description of the inner life of the mother Church appear to have been inserted by St Luke into another more general source. Such a source is indeed to be postulated, as St Luke was not an eye-witness of the earliest days of the Church. His working method here appears to be similar to that in the Third Gospel, where he enriched a document now lost with material taken from St Mark as well as from other sources.

　If this suggestion is accepted, we may confidently state that St Luke deliberately made a break after the story of Ananias and Sapphira. The reason for this break we have tried to find in our last lecture. He now sets out equally deliberately to reverse the story of the apparent success of St Peter and the Twelve. In two ways this is a very significant recognition. First it warns us against building any chronological edifice upon the book of Acts as we have it. St Luke's description of the events in the Jerusalem Church is not a chronological but an analytical one; he seeks to give the reasons for the course which it had to take. It may well be that the two events of the donation of St Barnabas and the faked donation of Ananias and Sapphira did not follow each other as closely as their record in Acts would suggest. Secondly we should understand that St Luke wished to indicate that the reverses of St Peter were neither due to lack of talent on his part nor to lack of guidance by the Holy Spirit, but rather part of the road which he, as the apostle of Jesus Christ, had to travel.

The connection of the short passage Acts 5:12–16 with the earlier narrative up to 3:11 is still a problem, because it is in itself disjointed; but it seems to us that if we bracket out 3:12–5:11, the transposing of verse 12a to the place suggested by Moffatt will prove unnecessary. He has tackled the task from the wrong end. That has also led him to an inaccurate translation of verse 13, which in his version runs: 'Though the people extolled them, not a soul from the outside dared to join them.' The Greek runs: 'but of the others nobody dared to join them, although the people extolled them.' That suggests to us that the narrative which St Luke used did not separate the many healings of verses 15–16 from the healing of the lame beggar, but gave to him only the distinction that he clung to the apostles. 'The others' in 5:13 are in fact the people whose cure is reported only in verses 15–16. St Luke did not want to omit this record of the many miraculous healings worked by the apostles, but stitched it on where it would do the least harm to the course of his story. These verses should be regarded as a kind of footnote.

We therefore regard the second arrest of 'the apostles' (verse 18), at the instigation of the high priest Annas and the Sadducees (verse 17), as a mere duplication, caused by the insertion of the passage Acts 3:12–5:11. However, the outcome of this arrest is different. The apostles are led into gaol and are miraculously delivered by an angel. This is an additional feature. Its importance is stressed by the fact that the persons arrested are not carefully described. We can say no more than that St Peter was among them. We find therefore that the Jerusalem Church had an old tradition that some of its prominent members, including St Peter, were led out of a closely locked and guarded prison by an angel. Evidently St Luke has twice made use of this tradition, here and in his report of St Peter's release from the prison of King Herod in Acts 12:6 f. Assuming that this is a duplication—and we cannot see any other reasonable approach to the problem—we must take notice that the intercession on behalf of St Peter on the latter occasion, offered by the whole Church (Acts 12:5), is omitted here. However, in Acts 4:24b–30 we have the very prayer of intercession which was used. In the place where it now stands it is obviously ill fitted to the situation after the release of St Peter and St John; but it would find its proper place after their arrest. This is just an illustration of how St Luke collected a certain amount of flotsam for his history of the early days of the Jerusalem Church, which he used in preference to inventing either sermons or circumstances of a miraculous character.

In contrast to the novellistic art of the authors of the apocryphal Acts he was a sober and serious historian.

II

Thus St Luke marked the next step on the way of the Church, the parting of ways of Christianity and Jewry. By the angelic intervention the apostles were sent from their gaol to the temple: 'Go and stand in the temple, telling the people all about this Life' (Acts 5:20), i.e. about the life eternal. Thus the claim for the control of the temple was given divine sanction; the words of Jesus weeping over Jerusalem (Luke 13:34), 'how often I would fain have gathered your children as a fowl gathers her brood under her wings', are heard here for the last time. This observation is important, for once it is made the analogies between the passion of Jesus and the treatment meted out to his disciples come to the fore. We will sum them up at once: first, the speech of Gamaliel (Acts 5:35 ff.) corresponds to Pilate's verdict (Luke 23:15), 'He has done nothing, you see, that calls for death; so I shall release Him with a whipping.' Secondly, the martyrdom of St Stephen and the subsequent persecution of the Church correspond to the intransigence of the Jewish populace at the passion and death of Jesus Christ. The whole meaning of the portion of Acts now under consideration is the repetition of the experience of our Lord in His body, the Church; and it thus reminds us of a saying of St Paul's (Col. 1:24, 25):

I am suffering now on your behalf, but I rejoice in that: I make up the full sum of all that Christ has to suffer in my flesh on behalf of the church, his Body. For I am a minister of the Church by the divine commission which has been granted me in your interest to make a full presentation of God's message.

This, we should say, is the structure of the portion of Acts from 5:12 to 7:60, which we now have under consideration.

This portion of Acts is clearly divided into three equal parts, the witness and trial of 'Peter and the apostles' (Acts 5:17–42); the appointment of St Stephen and the other six (Acts 6:1–15); and the sermon and martyrdom of St Stephen (7:1–60). These three parts we shall now proceed to analyse.

Beginning with the witness and trial of St Peter and the apostles, we would draw attention to the one outstanding fact that, although there is a large audience when they are found in the temple, St Luke refrains from inserting a sermon of St Peter or any other of the apostles. This seems to us an important observation. What better opportunity could there have been to invent a speech? However, we have already seen in the case of the healing of the lame beggar that these speeches were not the free invention of St Luke. Thus neither the miraculous release from prison is used by him for a further sermon nor the subsequent accusation by the high priest (Acts 5:28):

We strictly forbade you to teach about this Name, did we not? And here you have filled Jerusalem with your doctrine! You want to make us responsible for this man's death!

Nothing of this is said in any of St Peter's sermons. In fact, we remember clearly that in his address at the healing of the lame beggar he said (Acts 3:17):

Now I know, brothers, that you acted in ignorance, like your rulers.

Thus the accusation falls somewhat flat. Admittedly that would be a very clever way to put the high priest in the wrong if it were meant to show that it was his own bad conscience which caused this accusation, and not the preaching of the apostles; but we shall see that such was not the intention of St Luke. The fact is rather that he had no speech for this occasion, and that he did not invent one.

For the reply of St Peter (Acts 5:29 ff.) admits the accusation of the high priest.

One must obey God rather than men. The God of our fathers raised Jesus whom you had murdered by hanging him on a gibbet. God lifted him up to his right hand as our pioneer and saviour, in order to grant repentance and remission of sins to Israel.

This was not a sermon, but a credal formula of the binitarian type, of which a whole number is to be found in the New Testament. Interesting and to the point is the fact that the insertion 'hanging him on a gibbet' is an Old Testament quotation. It refers to Deut. 21:22 f.:

If any man has committed a sin deserving death, and if he is put to death and you have hanged him on a gibbet, his corpse must not remain all night on the gibbet, but you must lay it in a grave the same day.

The quotation is so pertinent, if it is to be assumed that Joseph of Arimathaea (Luke 23:50 f.) and perhaps also Nicodemus (John 3:1; 7:50; 19:39) were still members of the Sanhedrin. Jewish sources of rabbinical times at any rate revel in such undertones, and that makes us feel that St Luke even here drew upon an earlier source.

This source, we believe, also contained the speech of Gamaliel, which is of great significance. The speaker is described as 'a Pharisee in the Sanhedrin' (Acts 5:34), and he is mentioned again in Acts 22:3, as the teacher of St Paul. He is also known from Jewish, rabbinical sources as well as from Josephus. He was perhaps the grandson of the great founder of one of the two Pharisaic schools, Hillel, and certainly the grandfather of the first Jewish Patriarch after the fall of Jerusalem in A.D.70, whom we call Gamaliel II. Otherwise he is no more than a name. We have to judge him by what he says, and the gist of his speech is, 'wait and see'. The really remarkable thing about his speech is something negative. This speech of the leader of the Pharisaic party in the Sanhedrin contains not a single reference to the Old Testament. What Gamaliel gave was purely secular advice: this leader of the Pharisees is represented as being merely a politician. That comes out in his closing remarks (Acts 5:38, 39):

If this project or enterprise springs from men, it will collapse; whereas, if it really springs from God, you will be unable to put them down. You may even find yourselves fighting God!—

or, as 'D' says, from an experience of many years of state persecution:

neither you nor emperors nor tyrants will be able to put them down: therefore stay your hand with regard to these people.

The importance of these words is that they are meant to depict the Jewish agnostic. St Luke does not want us to admire the wisdom of Gamaliel. His aim is much rather to give an illustration to the words of his teacher St Paul in I Cor. 1:21:

For when the world with all its wisdom failed to know God in his wisdom, God resolved to save the believers by the 'sheer folly' of the Christian message.

Gamaliel is in fact neither wise nor generous in his approach to the apostles, but he imagines that he can be a mere onlooker, and thus—he misses the 'bus.

On the other hand it has to be stressed that the affair did not finish on this intellectual level. For the apostles were not dismissed with a caution only, but with that kind of admonition which was customary at the time, a whipping. I do not think that such treatment hurt people any less then than it would now. Nevertheless, there is a curiously ironical tinge in these two verses, Acts 5:40, 41. The sting is directed mainly against Gamaliel, as if St Luke would say: that is what his lofty ideals lead to; actual life is more brutal than his fine rhetoric. There is, on the other hand, something incongruous also in the description of the apostles, 'rejoicing that they had been considered worthy of suffering dishonour for the sake of the Name' (verse 41). Their suffering brings to mind St Paul's remark in II Cor. 4:17:

The slight trouble of the passing hour results in a solid glory past all comparison—

especially when it is compared with the martyrdom of St Stephen, which is to follow immediately. St Luke knew—and we assume that he did not wish to gloss it over—that St Peter and the other apostles were not to be the first martyrs of Christ; and his remark in Acts 5:41 is therefore either just a little flat, or it must be taken as a pointer to the fact that the apostles' time as leaders of the Jerusalem Church was drawing to a close: their end was not to be in Jerusalem.

III

The toleration of the Church by the Jewish authorities, which St Peter had obviously hoped to turn into a positive faith in Jesus Christ, was wearing very thin. From a worldly point of view his policy had failed. Inside the Church too his authority was challenged. That was only to be expected. For the Church had proved attractive, as Jesus had intended that it should, to the Jewish underdogs. There were numerous class distinctions in Palestine. Priests and scribes, Pharisees and Sadducees, townfolk and country-folk, Palestinian Jews and Jews of the dispersion, higher and lower degrees in Judaism right down to the 'devout' or God-fearing people looked askance at each other. Even among the Jews of the dispersion nationalities were carefully considered. Accepting Moffatt's emendation, we find in Acts 6:9

the so-called synagogue of the Libyans, the Cyrenians, and the Alexandrians, as well as . . . that of the Cilicians and Asiatics.

Taking these as five different groups we conclude that the Jews from the various parts of the Empire kept themselves to themselves even in Jerusalem, because they were not accepted into the circle of the indigenous Jerusalem people.

They were, however, received into the Church. No distinction was to be made between 'those who are afar off and those who are near'. At the same time old prejudices die hard. The Christians who were natives of Palestine and the 'Hellenists' were not easily to be joined in one, and the Hellenists complained. The apostles had to grant that the complaint was just, and arranged for an adequate representation because they would not themselves 'drop preaching the word of God and attend to meals' (Acts 6:2). The representatives were duly elected, seven men, all with Greek names, and the apostles appointed them with laying on of hands for their new position.

On the surface all this looks quite straightforward, and so it may have been. However, there are numbers of questions which we would like to have answered. The first and foremost is, where the apostles found the authority for this appointment of St Stephen and the other six? For up to this point they had guided the mother Church, as we have seen, in an almost hourly expectation of the second advent of Christ. Now, however, they suddenly began with the establishment of what looks very much like a more permanent administration. Had they changed their mind in the light of the experience with the Sanhedrin? The answer to this question will also throw light upon the conception of the Church held by St Luke and upon the origin of the rite of laying on of hands.

For this answer is to be found once more in the Old Testament, in Num. 11:16 f.:

The Eternal said to Moses: 'Gather seventy of the sheikhs of Israel, men whom you know to be sheikhs of the people and authorities; bring them to the Trysting tent, to stand beside you; I will come down and talk to you there, and I will endue them with part of your spirit; they shall share the burden of the people with you, instead of you bearing it by yourself.'

We know from the Talmud that the rabbis maintained that these seventy men were ordained with laying on of hands. We have therefore good reason to believe that this was the precedent for St Peter and the apostles' ordaining the Seven—instead of seventy—in the way in which they were ordained, with laying on of hands. We may also claim from this precedent that St Luke, at least from now on, wanted the Church to be understood as the new Israel on its pilgrimage through the wilderness.

There are further questions concerning the preference of the apostles to preach rather than to 'attend to meals'. Assuming that the common meals of the mother Church still preserved their sacramental character, it appears that the apostles gave preference to the ministry of the word over the ministry of the sacrament: but this question cannot be answered on the basis of Acts alone. There is also the question how it was that St Stephen was allowed to 'perform great wonders and miracles amongst the people' (Acts 6:8), whilst his commission was, as it appears, within the Church rather than to the people outside. For the context makes it quite clear that his activities were by no means confined to the people within the Church. To this question we will give first a preliminary answer, which is that this was a further development in the course of time. For Acts 6:7 clearly marks an interval in the narrative:

And the word of God spread; the number of the disciples in Jerusalem greatly increased, and a host of priests became obedient to the faith.

This short verse is meant to cover a further period of growth of an uncertain length of time during which no dramatic events occurred within the Jerusalem Church. It is not impossible that by it St Luke wanted to indicate that the rift between the Hebrews and the Hellenists, if it continued, was no longer of any significance, but this exegesis may put a little too much weight upon this verse. The real puzzle is the information about the numerous priests turning Christian. A suggestion which was thrown out some eighty years ago may deserve attention, namely that St Luke wanted to counterbalance St Stephen's attack upon the temple. We have seen how St Peter had claimed the temple for the true High Priest, Jesus Christ. It is attractive to think that numerous priests heeded his appeal; but that it was the party of the Jewish high priests, the Sadducees, which barred the way by which the temple might have been saved. What position, if any, these priests may have filled within the Church, we have no means to say. As they received no special consideration in the Jewish Synagogue after the destruction of the temple merely on account of their being of the family of Aaron, we are inclined to draw the same conclusion regarding the Church of Christ.

IV

So we come to the martyrdom of St Stephen. H. J. Cadbury is undoubtedly right in saying that the Greek names of the Seven by no means prove that they were actually Greeks. Only Nicolaus is described as a 'proselyte from Antioch' (Acts 6:6), which indicates that the others were probably born Jews. However, when we see that St Stephen's antagonists were Jews of the dispersion, we wonder whether he, 'being full of grace

31

and power' (Acts 6:8), may not have been the first to preach the gospel in the Greek language, a suggestion which does not detract anything from the miracle at Pentecost. Such an assumption may also make it easier to understand the relationship between the Seven and the Twelve. For it is somewhat puzzling that St Stephen at his trial never refers to the counsel of Gamaliel, although he stood before the same Sanhedrin that St Peter had had to face not so long ago, and that the high priest too seems to have forgotten it. His rather naïve question, 'Is this true?' (Acts 7:1) can hardly be construed as meaning that St Peter's views on the matter had been different. We would suggest, therefore, that the story of St Stephen comes from an independent source, which existed on its own.

This view conflicts with a widely held opinion that it was St Luke himself who added, rather sketchily, the accusation of St Stephen before the Sanhedrin, whereas actually he was lynched by the mob.[1] This view is supported by the allegation that St Luke intentionally omitted in his Gospel the accusation that Jesus himself had threatened to destroy the temple, because he wished to use it rather in connection with St Stephen. All this seems to us somewhat far-fetched. If we consider the part played by the mob at St Paul's trial (Acts 23:10), we feel that the distinction between trial by the Sanhedrin and lynching by the mob can easily be overdone. In any case the mob was, right from the beginning, present at St Stephen's trial (Acts 11, 12):

They then instigated people to say, 'We heard him talking blasphemy against Moses and God.' In this way they excited the people, the elders, and the scribes, who rushed on him, dragged him away, and took him before the Sanhedrin.

Thus the atmosphere was now completely changed. In the case of St Peter and St John the mob was siding with the apostles; therefore the Sanhedrin found itself greatly hampered with regard to the measures which it planned to take against them. In the case of St Stephen the mob finally took the law into its own hands; but by stoning him the people made it quite clear that an execution according to the law of Moses was envisaged. Finally, in the case of St Paul, no legal conclusion of any sort was reached; it went already far beyond the small affairs over which that unimportant community at the far corner of the Mediterranean could exercise its jurisdiction. Viewed from this angle, St Stephen formed the link between St Peter and St Paul, as he did in other respects also.

One such other aspect seems to be worth mentioning, because it leads up to the main subject of contention between St Stephen and the Jews:

[1] E. Meyer, *Ursprung und Anfänge des Christentums* iii (Berlin, 1923), p. 157.

the teaching of the Twelve took place in the portico of Solomon; that of St Stephen in the synagogues. Thus taking it locally St Peter's teaching could be regarded by the Jews as constructive criticism, whereas St Stephen's was disruptive. And so indeed it was. It is true that already Trito-Isaiah had said (Isa. 63:16):

Though Abraham may ignore us, though Israel regard us not, thou, O Eternal One, thou art our Father . . . —

and the Hellenistic Jews and proselytes were still greatly suspected by the Jerusalem crowds when they came to the temple, as St Paul's experience was going to prove once more.

Thus the temple was a questionable asset to the Jews of the dispersion. On the one hand they clung to it tenaciously. The sums to be sent to the Jerusalem temple by the Jews abroad caused headaches in Roman government circles more than once, and were undoubtedly a major political issue. On the other hand, those who went to Jerusalem and stayed there in between the festal periods found, as we have said already, a rather cold welcome. Therefore the temple assumed a somewhat questionable position in the minds of the Jews abroad, as may be seen from the fact that the one in Leontopolis in Egypt, to which the Pharisees objected rather strongly, had not only survived, but seems to have found a fairly strong adherence, certainly amongst non-Palestinian Jewry. The scene was indeed set for the separation of the Christian Church from the Jewish temple and this, so it appears, was also in the mind of St Luke when inserting at this place the sermon of St Stephen.

Foakes-Jackson in his commentary has treated the martyrdom and the sermon of St Stephen separately, making Acts 7:55–60 to follow immediately after 6:15.[1] That is a rather drastic operation and hardly to be commended. It is true that the sermon is very different in its content from the speeches found in the earlier Jewish 'Acts of Martyrs', which served as model for the martyrdom of St Stephen. However, it is equally true that a speech by the martyr was generally required. This speech should also contain an accusation of the unjust judge or judges before whom the martyr was arraigned. Both these conditions are complied with in our Acts of St Stephen, if it may be assumed that the Jewish nation as a whole was to be regarded as the judge in cases of blasphemy, where 'all the community must stone him' was the rule laid down by the Law (Lev. 24:16). In the same way, by reference to the pattern employed, the second alleged difficulty, which even Moffatt has marked by putting

[1] F. J. Foakes-Jackson, *The Acts of the Apostles* (London, 1931), pp. 87 f.

Acts 6:15 as a separate paragraph, is also removed. It was quite customary to describe in these 'Acts of Martyrs' the heavenly, inspired beauty of the martyr at the beginning of his speech. There is, therefore, no cogent reason to change anything in the description of St Stephen's martyrdom: we have the Acts of his martyrdom practically intact in Acts 6:8–7:60.

Regarding the sermon of St Stephen we have to confine ourselves to giving a short outline of it on the basis of that in Bruce's commentary.[1] In doing so we wish to make it clear that any attempts that have been made to show that the speech is not continuous are unavailing. Its construction is quite clear. It consists broadly speaking of two parts. The first part, 7:2–34, is meant to show by the examples of Abraham and Moses that God is not bound to any particular locality, but was with the chosen people on their pilgrimage from Mesopotamia to Palestine as well as from Palestine to Egypt and back again. Even the people themselves had in the days of the patriarchs not yet acquired any right to the Holy Land, with the exception of the grave of Abraham, which now lay in the territory of the despised and hated Samaritans, at Shechem (7:15, 16). The mention of Moses, the mediator of the old covenant, then introduces the second part, in that it brings to the preacher's mind the disobedience of the Israelites to his Law, which had been going on throughout their history right down to the judicial murder of Jesus Christ. The first part of the sermon was therefore intended to show that St Stephen had not committed any blasphemy when treating the temple with disrespect; and the second that his accusers and judges were in fact guilty of the very crime with which he was charged, because they had murdered 'the Just One' (Acts 7:52).

Several discrepancies are to be found between the account of the history of Israel in St Stephen's sermon and the facts to be derived from the Old Testament, and it also appears that the sermon does not always follow closely the text of the LXX (as in particular in verses 42, 43), but we cannot do more here than to state the fact. It is important, however, to emphasize the fact once more that the rabbis, successors of the Pharisees, denied unequivocally that God's Shekhinah, God's presence, had ever been in the post-exilic temple. This makes it clear that a remark addressed against the temple would not have been regarded by them as blasphemy worthy of death by stoning. It follows from this that St Stephen's attack upon the temple worship of his time was less far removed from the teaching of some of his Jewish contemporaries than might be

[1] F. F. Bruce, *The Acts of the Apostles* (London, 1952), pp. 160 ff.

deduced from its increasing fury. Nevertheless, he was led 'without the city wall' to be stoned.

St Stephen's martyrdom has often been compared with the passion of Jesus, and you will find the various analogies carefully enumerated in Foakes-Jackson's commentary.[1] They are indeed valid analogies, but the question remains what conclusions we have to draw from them. If we are not mistaken, these analogies result largely from the common model which was employed for the passion story in the Gospels as well as for the martyrdom of St Stephen, the early Jewish 'Acts of Martyrs'. Thus it may be well not to put too much stress on them. The last words of St Stephen, for instance, 'Lord Jesus, receive my spirit' (Acts 7:59, and 'Lord, let not this sin stand against them' (Acts 7:60), may indeed both be modelled upon St Luke's account of Jesus's passion (Luke 23:34, 46) and indicate that St Luke intended to draw a parallel between Jesus and His first martyr; but it must not be forgotten that 'Father, I trust my spirit into thy hands' (Luke 23:46) is a quotation from Ps. 31:5, which 'Lord Jesus, receive my spirit' is not, and that the sequence of the two sayings of Jesus is reversed in the martyrdom of St Stephen. The analogies between the Passion of Jesus and the martyrdom of St Stephen appear closer in English than they are in Greek.

Here for the first time Saul makes his appearance in a semi-official part, as prescribed in Deut. 17:7 ('The witnesses shall be the first to take a hand in killing him . . .'). This provides us with an occasion to ask the question, how far the report about St Stephen's martyrdom may be regarded as historically correct, for St Paul in his Epistles nowhere mentions his name. There are two great obstacles to surmount: the one in John 18:31, 'the Jews said, We have no right to put anyone to death' (which may perhaps be overcome—if St John's remark is historically correct—by the fact that no formal sentence was passed by the Sanhedrin on St Stephen), and the other and far weightier one, that St Luke's report is so thoroughly stylized. It tells us how a Christian martyr ought to die, as exemplified by St Stephen, and leaves out all the sordid details, enlarging on the edifying ones. If that in itself is a mark of untruth, then the story may be called unhistorical, although we cannot believe that such an event as St Stephen's martyrdom never occurred. If, however, as we believe, sordidness is not the mark of historical truth, the noble description of St Stephen's death will not make us doubt that he also died a noble death.

[1] *The Acts of the Apostles* (London, 1931), p. 58.

4 St Philip and the Mission to Samaria

If we claim that there is a real probability that St Luke, the companion of St Paul, was the author of the canonical book of Acts, we shall have to face up to the implications which such a statement involves. So far we have spoken vaguely of 'sources' for St Luke's narrative. We have, for instance, assumed that St Peter's sermon at the healing of the lame beggar had originally nothing to do with the event to which it is attached in Acts. We have also claimed that the 'Acts' of St Stephen's martyrdom existed originally as a separate document. We must now put the question, in what way St Luke came by the documents which he used for his description of the earliest days of the mother Church at Jerusalem.

The reason why we have to ask this question is the introduction of St Philip on the scene (Acts 8:5):

Philip travelled down to a town in Samaria, where he preached Christ to the people.

It is true that St Philip has been mentioned already in the list of the Seven (Acts 6:5), immediately after St Stephen, heading the 'other six'. However, in that context the distinction made between 'Stephen, a man full of faith and of the Holy Spirit', and the bare list of names, 'Philip, Prochorus, Nicanor, Timon, Parmenas and Nicolaus, a proselyte from Antioch', gives no indication of the considerable part to be played by St Philip in the progress of St Luke's narrative: but in chapter 8 he appears as the chief character, and in 21:8 he is once more introduced, and this time as a personal acquaintance of both St Paul and St Luke:

We ... started next morning for Caesarea, where we entered the house of Philip the evangelist (he belonged to the Seven, and had four unmarried daughters who prophesied). We stayed with him. While we remained there for a number of days, a prophet called Agabus came down from Judaea.

There was, therefore quite a reunion of old acquaintances, for Agabus too had been mentioned earlier, in Acts 11:27 f.:

During these days some prophets came down from Jerusalem to Antioch, one of whom, named Agabus, showed by the Spirit that a severe famine was about to visit the whole world.

We are given to understand there that he made the acquaintance of St Paul already on this occasion, whilst we gather from Acts 21:10, that St Luke came to know him only at the house of St Philip.[1]

Let us consider Agabus first, for there is far less to say about him. The identity of the Agabus in 11:27 f. with the one in 21:10 seems beyond question, but it is, of course, possible that St Luke had his information about his prophecy from St Paul. However, it seems to us that the insertion about his prophecy in Acts 11:27 f. comes somewhat unexpectedly, as if it were a piece of information picked up by accident which appeared too valuable to be suppressed, but which originated from a different source. We feel very little hesitation in ascribing it to the personal meeting of St Luke and Agabus. If this suggestion is accepted, however, there would then be some evidence that the stay of St Paul and his friends at Caesarea offered St Luke an opportunity of collecting evidence about the history of the Church in the time before he became a Christian.

From this recognition we proceed to the far more important question whether St Philip also acted as a source of information for St Luke. We can state as certain that the opportunity for doing so was offered at their meeting at Caesarea. There are, however, several difficulties to overcome, before we can reach any conclusion. First, we should be clear about who this St Philip was. For if it were true that the writer of Acts himself had no clear idea about him, our case would fall to the ground. St Philip is described in Acts 21:8 as 'the evangelist' and as one of the Seven, and this is generally understood to mean that he was not an apostle; and since in Acts 1:13 the name of St Philip is mentioned as one of the Twelve, the conclusion has been generally drawn that there were two St Philips, of whom one was a member of the Twelve and the other a member of the Seven. This conclusion seems to be fortified by Eph. 4:11:

He granted some men to be apostles, some to be prophets, some to be evangelists, some to shepherd and teach. . . .

To this may also be added II Tim. 4:5:

do your work as an evangelist, and discharge all your duties as a minister.

For since Timothy was certainly no apostle, and since apostles, prophets and evangelists are distinguished in Eph. 4:11, it is concluded that if the St Philip of Acts 21:8 had been a member of the Twelve, St Luke would not have described him as 'the evangelist'.

---

[1] The 'D' editor, by giving 11:28 the form of a 'we' report, makes Luke present on the occasion of Agabus's earlier appearance.

This argument has some weight, but less than appears, for two reasons: The first is that both Ephesians and II Timothy are rather late productions which presuppose a much more elaborate Church organization than Acts. The second is that the early Church only remembered one St Philip. We have several references to him in documents inserted by Eusebius in his *Ecclesiastical History*. Clement of Alexandria, who knew Acts, also refers to him; and all these testimonies know only of one St Philip and incidentally know nothing of his being one of the Seven. On the other hand, in John 12:21, 22, it is St Philip to whom the Greeks apply who want to see Jesus. We also hear from one of Eusebius's witnesses, the bishop Polycrates of Ephesus, that St Philip the apostle was buried together with his two maiden daughters who had been prophetesses at Hierapolis in Asia Minor (one of the cities of the Lycus valley mentioned by St Paul in Col. 4:13). Only the story of the Seven finds no corroboration from outside sources.

Thus we come to two conclusions. The one is that there was never a suggestion of two St Philips in the early Church, before Acts was misunderstood in that way. The second is that, although the martyrdom of St Stephen was remembered in the early Church, his position in the Jerusalem Church would have been forgotten, had it not been preserved in Acts. So much is certain. As a hypothesis we may add that the whole ministry of the Seven can have lasted only for a very short time. That is suggested by the fact that, as G. B. Caird has pointed out,[1] the conversion of St Paul must have happened in A.D. 35 at the latest, more probably in A.D. 34, so that for the whole history of the Church at Jerusalem up to St Stephen's death we have at best three years. To belong to the Seven was not an appointment for life. It appears to us that St Luke wanted to indicate his source for the incident of the Seven when he described St Philip as 'one of the Seven'. That story was new, even to the majority of the members of the former Jerusalem Church, when St Luke composed Acts; and they were dispersed probably over all the world after the fall of Jerusalem in A.D. 70. St Luke's source for the story, therefore, was St Philip, and we may assume that he also gave St Luke an account of his own subsequent experiences.

If we thus claim St Philip as an authority for St Luke's report, we must not assume that he was his only authority; for we have already seen that the martyrdom of St Stephen was a written document which had come independently into St Luke's hands. This will also prove true with regard to the early ministry of St Philip. There are, as we will see, two sources

[1] *The Apostolic Age* (London, 1955), pp. 198 ff.

to be distinguished in chapter 8 of Acts. However, before we proceed to analyse this chapter, we have to answer two more questions; one incidental and the other of great significance for the whole intention of St Luke's work. The one is, why St Luke called St Philip 'the evangelist', but did not describe him further as a member of the Twelve; the other is, why St Luke did not give us any more of St Philip's experiences?

The answer to the first question is easy. If there was only the one St Philip who was known to the early Christians, then his membership in the council of the Twelve was also well known amongst them, and its mention at this juncture when St Paul returned to Jerusalem for the last time might have caused a lot of unnecessary questions. The Twelve were human beings like others, and it is no more than a pious wish that they should not have quarrelled. In fact the Gospel records show that they did do so already when their Master was among them. Theologically the Twelve were not an earthly, but an eschatological ministry, as is shown by their attendance at the ascension. To be a member of the Twelve was not of necessity a distinction upon earth, as soon as the pentecostal period of the Church was passed. St Peter, for instance, describes himself as a presbyter (I Pet. 5:1). There is far too much imagination wasted on the presumptive authority which the Twelve may or may not have enjoyed in the early Church. As a group they are not mentioned anywhere after the resurrection, except in the early chapters of Acts and in I Cor. 15:5. There too their distinction lay in a special visitation by the risen Lord, and the mention of them in Acts 6:2, which has caused uneasiness amongst New Testament scholars before, is most probably due to St Luke's faithful reproduction of St Philip's report. Thus 'the evangelist' was probably meant to give a description of St Philip's earthly work, something which even the word 'apostle' would not necessarily convey.

If this answers our first question, the second one, why we hear so little in Acts about the exploits of St Philip, may be answered best with the title of a long forgotten book by the German scholar Wilhelm Erbt, *From Jerusalem to Rome*,[1] who incidentally advanced a theory, accepted by only a very small number of scholars, that Acts consisted of a first half written by St Mark and a second written by St Luke—a very instructive book, although mistaken in its conclusions. For this book insists most strongly upon the fact that St Luke had the intention to describe the spreading of the gospel of Jesus Christ from the spiritual

[1] *Von Jerusalem nach Rom* (Berlin, 1896).

centre of the old covenant, Jerusalem, to the political centre of the world, Rome, and that it left out all bye-ways. The verse Acts 1:8—

you will receive power when the Holy Spirit comes upon you, and you will be my witnesses, throughout all Judaea and Samaria, and to the end of the world—

is, according to this book, the theme of the book of Acts, and we believe that that is undoubtedly correct. In that case 'the evangelist' Philip was, as also the non-canonical sources describe him, a well-known missioner; but his field of action touched the straight route from Jerusalem to Rome only in one point, Samaria.

II

Samaria presents a special problem to the New Testament student. We have already quoted Matt. 10:5 f., 'do not go among the Gentiles and do not enter a Samaritan town; rather make your way to the lost sheep of the house of Israel', in a previous lecture. Let us repeat that this saying is only found in the First Gospel, where it also receives support from the story of the Syro-Phoenician woman. For whereas this story as such is also reported in Mark 7:24 f., the words, 'it was only to the lost sheep of the house of Israel that I was sent', are found only in Matt. 15:24, and are an obvious addition. It may well be that the comparatively late Gospel according to St Matthew shows that a hardening of heart towards the mission among the non-Jews took place within Judaeo-Christian circles, especially with regard to St Philip's mission to the Samaritans. We have already hinted at dissensions among the Twelve, and it is certainly most remarkable that St Philip, even after the persecution of the Church had died down at Jerusalem, did not return there, but settled down at the Gentile centre in Palestine, at Caesarea (Acts 8:40; 21:8). It is also significant in this respect that in St Stephen's sermon (Acts 7:16) there is to be found an alteration of the report of Gen. 33:19 and Josh. 24:32, that *Israel* bought the ground for his tomb from the sons of Hamor in Shechem, to *Abraham's* buying it. For Abraham, according to Gen. 23:16 ff., bought the ground for his grave from Ephron the Hittite near Mamre, which is Hebron in Southern Judaea.

It will therefore be worth our while to cast a glance at the general attitude of the Gospels with regard to the Samaritans. In the Second Gospel neither Samaria nor the Samaritans are mentioned. In the Gospel according to St Luke we have on the one hand the story of St James and St John who suggest destroying the Samaritan village which would not receive Jesus on His pilgrimage from Galilee to Jerusalem (Luke 9:51 ff.) and on the other the story of the good Samaritan in Luke 10:25 ff., and the story of the ten lepers in Luke 17:11 ff. This survey seems to indicate a deep-seated aversion against the Samaritans on the part of the Twelve, and a campaign on their behalf by their Master. In contrast to this the First Gospel (Matt. 10:23) records the saying of Jesus, 'truly, I tell you, you will not have covered the towns of Israel before the Son of man arrives', as an explanation of his forbidding the disciples to enter any Samaritan town (10:6). Finally, the Fourth Gospel gives by far the major part of its fourth chapter to Jesus's own mission amongst the Samaritans, and records (John 8:48) that the Jews even accused Jesus himself of being a Samaritan. It has to be remembered, however, that the Fourth Gospel in Jesus's dialogue with the Samaritan woman at Jacob's well makes the explicit statement, 'salvation comes from the Jews' (John 4:22). Thus the Gospels, historically arranged, witness to the fact that there was a vivid discussion about the preaching of the gospel to the Samaritans going on in the early Church.

The Samaritan question was actually a Jewish one, which had arisen after the return of the Jews from the Babylonian exile, when Nehemiah separated the Jews and the Samaritans (Neh. 4:1 ff.). The Samaritans claimed to be true Israelites, left behind in their country after the destruction of the kingdom of Israel, whereas Jewish tradition (II Kings 17:24 ff.) had it that they were a mixed race, consisting of five different elements, who had accepted a hybrid Israelite priesthood (verses 27 f.), to satisfy the God who was the Master of the country to which they had been sent. Scholars seem now to be agreed that there is more to be said in favour of the Samaritan claim than biblical evidence would allow; but this question need not worry us. Important, however, is the fact that, like the Jews, the Samaritans expected the coming of a Saviour, the so-called *Ta'eb*, basing their hopes upon the very verses, Deut. 18:15 ff., which St Peter after the healing of the lame beggar at the Beautiful Gate had used in his sermon (Acts 3:22 f.) They were, therefore, prepared to accept the Christ, if only the Christians would preach him to them.

Yet it took a catastrophe like the martyrdom of St Stephen and the first persecution of the Church to bring St Philip to Samaria. Where exactly he went we do not know. If we accept the reading of Acts 8:5, 'to *the* city of Samaria', it would be Sebaste, the capital of the district, but the good witnesses are almost equally divided for and against this reading.

D

St Luke may not have remembered the name of the town. If we were entitled to use the evidence of John 4:6, it would be Sychar on the slope of mount Gerizim, near Jacob's grave. If the reference to Simon Magus is used as a pointer, it might be Gitta which, according to Justin Martyr, was Simon's native town. The matter is, however, of no great importance.

What is of very real significance is the fact that the crowds in Samaria were willing to listen to the 'Hellenist' Philip. It has often—and rightly—been stated that Acts 8:7—

For unclean spirits came screaming and shrieking out of many who had been possessed, and many paralytics and lame people were healed—

appears as a replica of Acts 5:16:

bringing invalids and people troubled with unclean spirits, all of whom wer e healed.

In a lesser degree this may be also said of the description of St Paul's miracles on Malta (Acts 28:9):

the rest of the sick folk in the island also came and got cured.

Again we have to ask what significance should be attached to these similarities. One might say that they point to the special interest of St Luke, the physician, in miraculous cures; but going through the article *therapeuein*, to heal, in a reliable Greek concordance of the New Testament has shown that the number of cases in which that word is used in St Matthew is greater than even in Luke and Acts together. It seems rather that St Luke wanted to illustrate the doctrine of his teacher St Paul, who in II Cor. 12:9,

it is in weakness that my power is fully felt,

gives the key to this parallelism. St Peter, just about to be arrested; St Philip, a fugitive from the persecution at Jerusalem; St Paul, 'the prisoner of the Lord', all show God's power of healing and thus proclaim Christ the Saviour sent by Him.

It was, of course, also in order to confound Simon Magus that St Philip was granted the power of healing by Jesus Christ. For Simon had been 'practising magic arts in the town to the utter astonishment of the Samaritan nation' (Acts 8:9). Here we must enter upon what scholars of the last four generations have styled the Simon Magus legend.[1] Who

[1] Cf. A. Ehrhardt, *The Framework of the New Testament Stories* (Manchester, 1964), pp. 161 ff.

was this Simon Magus? Let it be said forthwith that we know of him only from Christian sources, which may be divided into three groups. The first consists of certain Fathers of the Church. Justin Martyr, who died a martyr's death at Rome in ±A.D. 165, has already been mentioned. He denounced the school of Simon Magus to the Roman authorities as a dangerous heresy. This warning was taken up by Irenaeus of Lyons and Hippolytus of Rome who, at the turning of the second to the third century, warned Christians of his heresy, stating that Simon was the originator of Christian gnosticism. The second group consists of the apocryphal Acts of St Peter, written during the second century in Asia Minor, which describes the duel of miracles between St Peter and Simon Magus at Rome, at the end of which Simon tried to fly up in the air, but crashed and died. Finally the third group consists of the so-called Pseudo-Clementines. They record the chase of St Peter after Simon Magus through Syria. They are a production of the Church at Antioch and are distinguished by the fact that they furnish Simon with features of St Paul. All these sources are of second-century origin, and are therefore not to be taken as better information than Acts 8:9 ff., which is of first-century origin.

The question is whether the story about Simon Magus in Acts 8:9–13 is of any historical value, or should be regarded as being legendary too. The most that can be adduced in favour of the report in this paragraph being legendary is the description of Simon as 'that power of God which is known as "the Great Power" ' (Acts 8:10). Confirmation of this, however, comes not only from Lucian, the second-century satirist, in his biography of the 'lying prophet', Alexander of Abunoteichos, but also from a biography of Apollonius of Tyana, a philosopher and miracle-worker of the first century, written by one Philostratus of the third century. We also hear of similar miracle workers connected with the Christian Church from the greatest opponent of Christianity, the Platonic philosopher Celsus; and finally we know of one Menander, a Samaritan, who is described to us by Irenaeus of Lyons and Hippolytus of Rome as a Christian gnostic as well as a pupil of Simon Magus. We therefore find no difficulty in accepting the statement that Simon Magus was baptized by St Philip as historically true. Even more, we find in this report the historical basis of the saying ascribed to Jesus in John 4:22, 'salvation comes from the Jews'. There was much mysticism abroad in the first century, comparable to the mysticism of the eighteenth century. Samaria especially was riddled with it; but the Samaritans had to be taught—and accepted—the truth that their own workers of miracles were not incarnations of God, even though there were numerous claimants for this title among them. (Already before Simon Magus there is said to have been one Dositheus, who is represented to us by the Church Fathers as Simon's teacher.) The most famous representative of this group, Simon Magus, is said to have accepted this truth; but it is at least an open question whether he would have become so famous if he had not been baptized by St Philip.

However, these men were doubtful acquisitions for the Christian Church. We read in Mark 9:38 ff. = Luke 9:49 f., of St John's question:

'Teacher, we saw a man casting out daemons in your name; but he does not follow us, and so we stopped him.' Jesus said, 'Do not stop him; no one who performs any miracle in my name will be ready to speak evil of me. He who is not against us is for us.'

But we read also in Matt. 12:30 = Luke 11:23:

He who is not with me is against me, and he who does not gather with me scatters—

and we notice with interest that the earliest Gospel has only the comprehensive approach to all those who invoke the name of Jesus; that the latest of the three Synoptic Gospels has only the exclusive approach, whereas St Luke has both. In the case of Simon Magus an application shows, therefore, that there was a chance of a real conversion, whereas the sons of the Jewish priest Sceva (Acts 19:14) received the scornful reply of the evil spirit which they attempted to exorcize 'in the name of Jesus':

Jesus I know and Paul I know, but you—who are you?

We touch thus in the story of Simon Magus upon the beginnings of the 'Catholic' Church—as opposed to heretical bodies—and that is its significance in this context of Acts. At Jerusalem there was no question of heresy: Ananias and Sapphira were no heretics, and St Peter and St Stephen, although their appreciation of the temple varied so greatly, were both orthodox. However, as soon as the Church transcended the borders of Judaea, the question of heresy arose. It was the question how far pagan elements could be assimilated by the Christian proclamation of the Gospel, or had to be resisted. The standard by which this question was decided was the Old Testament.

III

Here the Jerusalem Church asserted its rights, and it is a Jerusalem source which provided the paragraph Acts 8:14–24. That can be proved by an analysis of the language, which is rather different from that in Acts 8:4–13 but it appears also from the fact that St Philip is not even mentioned in verses 14–24, as well as from the sudden change in the character of Simon Magus. In Acts 8:13 we hear:

Simon himself believed, and after his baptism kept close to Philip, utterly astonished to see the signs and striking miracles which were taking place.

We are thus given no reason to doubt his sincerity, neither is there any reason to believe that St Philip's baptism was in any respect less complete or less valid than that of the Jerusalem Church. However, 'the apostles at Jerusalem heard that Samaria had accepted the word of God'—no mention of St Philip—and they sent, in order to assert their authority over the new community, once more St Peter and St John.

The instruction which we are given here is as enlightening as it is unexpected. Only from this incident do we learn that the persecution at Jerusalem was not directed against 'the apostles', and that they continued at Jerusalem safely, whilst the friends of St Stephen were scattered (Acts 8:4), and that Saul, making 'havoc of the Church by entering one house after another, dragging off men and women, and consigning them to prison' (Acts 8:3), directed his activities against his fellow-Hellenists. Once it is realized that the action of the apostles in dispatching St Peter and St John to Samaria is at all questionable, it begins to smell of that policy on the part of the Jerusalem Church which was denounced by St Paul in Gal. 2:4,

There were traitors of false brothers, who had crept in to spy out the freedom we enjoy in Christ Jesus,

and by the reference to the 'certain emissaries of James' (Gal. 2:12).

There was yet one justification for the interference of St Peter and St John (Acts 8:15):

who came down and prayed that the Samaritans might receive the holy Spirit. (As yet he had not fallen on any of them; they had simply been baptized in the name of the Lord Jesus.)—

namely that they were to bring the gift of the Holy Spirit. All the same, the explanation of this verse is very difficult. For in Acts 2:38 after the miracle of Pentecost St Peter invited the Jews:

Repent, . . . let each of you be baptized in the name of Jesus Christ for the remission of your sins; then you will receive the gift of the holy Spirit.

There was then no suggestion that 'the gift of the Holy Spirit' could not be obtained by baptism 'in the name of the Lord Jesus' alone. We therefore are compelled to conclude that St Luke either did not tell us all he knew about the visit of the two apostles to Samaria, or else did not know himself all that was going on behind the scenes. Since, however, the story in Acts 8:26–40 is evidently St Philip's again, we prefer the first alternative. St Peter and St John were at that time 'the pillars', as St Paul calls them (Gal. 2:9), of the Jerusalem Church; but St James of Jerusalem, 'the brother of the Lord' (Gal. 1:19), already made his weight felt. He had strong connections with Jerusalem, which especially St Peter, the Galilean fisherman, had not, and he was also made of sterner stuff than St Peter.

The answer to our question cannot be found just by interpreting Acts 8:15; the whole situation rather calls for a realization of the fact that there were currents and counter-currents. The apostles came to receive the Samaritans into the Church, the only one of which they knew, the Church of Jerusalem; and to receive them not as partners, but as simple entrants. Simon Magus, however, demurred at their demand. The 'laying on of hands' signified in this case the reception of the Samaritans into the Church of the Spirit, the pentecostal Church at Jerusalem. The signs of the Spirit, we are given to understand, were made evident at the laying on of hands by the apostles, and Simon is said to have wanted to acquire that faculty for money. He wanted, so we should understand this, to become equal to the apostles, and form his own Samaritan Church which would be tributary to the Church at Jerusalem. For it is to be inferred that a Church had to be led by an apostle, and St Philip apparently was—only St Philip. Thus Simon received the curse of St Peter instead of his blessing (Acts 8:20–23). This, however, he accepted with an unexpected humility expressed in his beautiful reply (Acts 8:24):

Beseech the Lord for me! Pray that nothing you have said may befall me!

I confess to a feeling that Simon comes out much better from this encounter with the apostles than the tempestuous St Peter, who gives him no word of consolation; and I feel also that here is a puzzle to be solved. The Church lost a man here, who might have been saved;

St Peter trampled down the new plantation of St Philip, and Acts 8:25 appears as no more than a conciliatory addition by St Luke, to smooth out the discord between the two reports about the mission to Samaria which lay before him. It seems evident that he had to add the Jerusalem report, because he knew that the Church at Jerusalem gained the ascendancy over St Philip in Samaria. To make this clear we have to quote the last verse where the Samaritan Church is mentioned (Acts 9:31):

Now, all over Judaea, Galilee, and Samaria, the church enjoyed peace; it was consolidated, inspired by reverence for the Lord and by its invocation of the holy Spirit, and so increased in numbers.

This verse makes it clear that the new Israel of the Church of Jesus Christ had succeeded in bringing the whole kingdom of David under the sway of his Son's sceptre, something the Jews had tried, with much less success, by force of arms during the last five hundred years.

IV

It is, however, suggestive that St Luke separated this remark so far from his report on the visit of the two apostles to Samaria. For it was not for them to be altogether triumphant. St Philip had yet another poser to set for the heads of the new Israel, the Church. In order that we should realize the significance of the following event, once more an angelic vision is introduced by St Luke. The angels are used by him, it seems, in various cases as an exclamation mark, and that has been overlooked by all those interpreters who, on account of this angelic vision, deny the possibility of St Philip himself being the source of Acts 8:26 ff. As if nobody had ever said, 'I am sure it must have been an angel warning me.'

The special significance of this passage lies in the unequivocal commandment of Deut. 23:1:

No eunuch, no man sexually mutilated, shall enter the gathering (LXX *ekklēsia*) of the Eternal.

Already at the time of the prophets the harshness of this commandment had been resented, and Trito-Isaiah in his eschatological vision had proclaimed (Isa. 56:3 ff.):

Let not your foreigner say, 'The Eternal will excommunicate me'; let not your eunuchs say, 'Ah, we are but a barren tree.' For this is the Eternal's word: 'eunuchs who keep my sabbaths, who choose what I approve, and hold fast to my compact, theirs is a monument within my temple nobler than any sons or daughters, a memorial from myself that never shall be moved'.

We have seen how the promise made to the 'foreigner'—'for salvation comes from the Jews'—had been strained by the Jerusalem Church: the Samaritans had been brought into subjection instead of partnership by the apostles. What was the reply of the Jerusalem Church going to be with regard to the eunuch? Would it be realized in his case that by the coming of the Messiah the fulfilment of the Law had come about, and that he had broken the bar between Israel and the people outside?

The story itself is quite simple: St Philip is sent by the angel to the road from Jerusalem to Gaza, leading south-west. Where St Philip was at the time when he received this order is not told us, but it appears that the baptism of the eunuch did not follow immediately after the conversion of the Samaritans. In order to make room for the Jerusalem report, St Luke has suppressed part of Philip's story. The contrasting of the two events is his. St Philip is sent to 'the desert route' (Acts 8:26). The translation is not certain, but probable. He finds the eunuch sitting in his chariot, reading the 'song of the suffering Servant' (Isa. 53:7 f.), the very words which accompanied Jesus on his way to his passion. You all know that people read aloud in those days. He is invited at his inspired question, 'Do you really understand what you are reading?' (Acts 8:30), to join the eunuch's seat, and 'preached the gospel of Jesus to him' (Acts 8:35). Finally the eunuch is baptized. At his baptism no baptismal confession is demanded of him. Acts 8:37 is a later insertion, and rightly omitted not only by Moffatt, but also by the R.V. and R.S.V.

This is a dramatic situation, and the stage seems to be set for the great discussion between the Jerusalem Church and the mission churches. However, once more the Holy Spirit intervened. St Philip was whisked away by Him to Azotus (Acts 8:40), never, as far as we know, to return to Jerusalem at all. The stage was indeed set for the great drama of the Church's expansion all over the world, but the protagonist was not to be St Philip, but the persecutor of him and his fellow-Hellenists, Saul of Tarsus; and the antagonist was not to be St Peter, but St James of Jerusalem.

5   The Rise and Rule of James of Jerusalem

I

In Acts 1:14 we read how the Eleven returned after the Ascension from the Mount of Olives to Jerusalem, and 'resorted with one mind to prayer, together with the women (their wives), with Mary the mother of Jesus and with his brothers'. We have stated how this earliest Christian community already contained two different groups of potential leaders, the apostles on the one hand, and the house of David on the other. We have also seen how St Peter took the lead at the elevation of St Matthias to the chair vacated by Judas, and again at Pentecost and for the subsequent period, until the stoning of St Stephen and the ensuing persecution shook the young Church to its foundations. That is true, although St Luke very discreetly intimates to us that 'the apostles', in spite of the persecution, contrived to stay in Jerusalem. It appeared that the Jewish authorities were ready to distinguish between the Palestinian group of Christians and the foreigners of Jewish persuasion who had embraced the new faith. In order to understand this wariness on the part of the Jewish government, which had little sympathy for any brand of Christianity, we must try to go more intimately into the circumstances of the Christians at Jerusalem.

The persecution, even if it did not touch St Peter and the other Eleven —and we have made bold to suggest that it affected at least one of them, St Philip—was nevertheless a disaster for the young Church at Jerusalem in that it showed that it was if not unwilling yet certainly unable to protect the Hellenists who had embraced the new faith. The emotion at Jerusalem had proved too strong. We have in Acts 19:23 f. a report of the reaction amongst the people at Ephesus when they felt that their temple of Artemis (Diana) was threatened by the rise of the new Christian faith. The whole city rose in riot, for this new faith was a threat to those ideal possessions of the town which, at the same time, were known to be of the highest commercial value to its citizens. Generally the alliance between ideals and money is at the same time the most treacherous for those who side with it, and the most dangerous to attack for its opponents. It makes for such a damnably good conscience amongst its defenders.

This selfsame alliance also ruled the hearts and minds of the Jews at Jerusalem. Their temple was their idol, and St Stephen was defeated by this idol worship. The disparagement of the temple in his preaching threatened the chief trade of Jerusalem, the tourist industry, and thus almost all tradespeople, with ruin, and also blasphemed their most sacred convictions. St Peter's approach had been different. All the same, he and the other Eleven too lost much of their popular support. A few years later, in A.D. 43, the execution of St James, the son of Zebedee, at the orders of Herod Agrippa I, and the imprisonment of St Peter were going to be two very popular events, and that was then the only popularity left to them.

Nevertheless, the Church at Jerusalem not only survived the disaster of the persecution of the Hellenists, but even continued to have a decisive influence upon the affairs of the Church throughout the eastern half of the Roman Empire. There must have been some very strong and determined personality to take the helm when St Peter relinquished it. More than that, we have to look for a strong group of Jerusalem people using both influence and energy in order to safeguard the continuance of the Church at Jerusalem. The man for whom we have to look in this connection is mentioned in the New Testament, yet hardly more than mentioned by name. It is James of Jerusalem. What we have to find out are two things: what manner of man he was, and in what way he managed to secure for himself the rulership over the Church at Jerusalem. In both respects much that we will have to say will remain hypothetical. For St Luke was far less concerned with the history of the Jerusalem Church under James than with its earlier history. After all, that later history of the Church at Jerusalem was a closed episode when he composed the Acts of the Apostles; James as well as his successor Simeon had died a martyr's death, and the holy city had been destroyed by the Romans. Much animosity, so it seems, had also died with them.

It is perhaps the greatest loss for the historian of the Primitive Church, that he is told so little about the relations that existed between Jesus and his family. St Paul's remark (II Cor. 5:16), 'even though we have known Christ after the flesh, yet now we know him so no more' (Moffatt's translation[1] is to be rejected) has come true at least in so far as his family

[1] 'even though I once estimated Christ by what is external, I no longer estimate him thus'.

is concerned. Only the story in Mark 3:31-35 with its parallels in Matthew and Luke, ending with the saying (Mark 3:34 f.),

There are my mother and my brothers! Whoever does the will of God, that is my brother and sister and mother,

gives a hint at the tension that seems to have existed between him and them. For the other reference to Jesus's family (Mark 6:3 = Matt. 13:55),

Is this not the joiner, the son of Mary and brother of James and Joses and Judas and Simon? Are not his sisters settled here among us?

comes from third parties and can only be understood in the sense that his family were absent at the incident described for reasons unknown. Still more difficult is the assessment of John 7:5 with its categorical statement, 'for even his brothers did not believe in him'. Have we to take this statement as historically true for the time before the resurrection of Jesus Christ, or is it to be understood as a criticism of the Judaeo-Christian creed held by James and his nephew and successor, Simeon of Jerusalem? Is that Simeon by any chance to be identified with the Simon mentioned in Mark 6:3? We feel greatly tempted to claim that that is at least probable; but once more we have no means by which certainty in this matter might be reached. That is all the more tantalizing since it seems that the book of Bishop Papias of Hierapolis, of the first half of the second century, which might have enlightened us in all these matters, was still in existence at the beginning of the last century at the old Sultan's palace, since destroyed by fire, at Istanbul.

Thus we are at least doubtful about the attitude of Jesus's brothers during His ministry. On the other hand, St Luke makes it quite clear that they belonged to the earliest Christian community already before Pentecost. There can also be no doubt that St James of Jerusalem is to be included in this group, since St Paul (I Cor. 15:7) reports that the risen Lord had appeared to him. What has to be discussed is the question whether or not they were sons of Mary. This question is an open one largely because so many Christians, including myself, will not believe it. Two arguments against this assumption that they were Mary's children may be adduced. The first is derived from the Word from the Cross in John 19:26, 27, because if Jesus commended his mother in the way he did to his favourite disciple, she either had no other son, or else her other sons were still opposed to Jesus. Since, however, St Paul (I Cor. 15:7) reports that the risen Lord appeared to James, this latter possibility seems to be excluded. The second, weaker argument is that in Acts 1:14, 'with Mary the mother of Jesus, and with his brothers', a distinction seems to be introduced between 'the mother of Jesus' on the one hand, and 'his brothers' on the other.

These considerations are not only of general interest, but contribute to the picture of St James of Jerusalem, 'James the Just', as he was called by his followers. Even if Mary was not his mother, their relationship must have been close, for it seems that it was Mary who had connections of importance in Jerusalem. She was, according to Luke 1:36, 39–56, a relation of Elizabeth, the wife of Zechariah, a priest at the Jerusalem temple. It has also been suggested that 'Mary, the mother of John Mark' (Acts 12:12), at whose house the Christians met for prayer on behalf of St Peter in prison, might be identified with 'her sister, Mary the wife of Clopas' (John 19:25) or was at least a relation of hers or of James's. In short, as we have observed already in a previous lecture, the family of Jesus had closer connections with Jerusalem than the Galilean fisherman St Peter. Peter was a stranger there. Already at his denial of Jesus it had only been by the good services of 'another disciple', commonly but perhaps wrongly identified with St John, who was an acquaintance of the high priest (John 18:15), that St Peter gained admission to the high priest's house. Thus St Peter was an outsider; St James, however, so it appears, was not.

All the same, it took several years before St James succeeded first in gaining the ascendancy over St Peter and finally in ousting him. The first sign of the change we have found in the legation of St Peter and St John to the Samaritans. Obviously, as long as St Peter was the unrivalled head of the Jerusalem Church, he would not have been 'despatched' by it, as Acts 8:14 says, however important the occasion, but would either have gone of his own accord or would have sent somebody else. Although the name of St James is not mentioned it seems evident that he was now in control and not St Peter. Perhaps we can say even more: not only was St Philip glad to leave Jerusalem behind, but also St Peter. It appears that he was not sorry to watch things from a distance. Such is at any rate the impression created by the wording of Acts 9:32, that he 'moved here and there among them all'.

II

The Church in Judaea, outside Jerusalem, and the Church at Jerusalem were, it seems, joined together by organization. They were controlled centrally by a council of the apostles and elders at Jerusalem. Nevertheless, since the temple at Jerusalem played such a part in the worship there, the Church life in places like Lydda and Jaffa must have been very different from that at Jerusalem. It is well known that the formation of the Christian liturgy was largely dependent on forms of worship which were used in the Jewish synagogues of the day, and we can safely state that the Church in Judaea must be more responsible for this similarity than that at Jerusalem. We have also reason to assume that the Galilean St Peter felt more at home in these Christian synagogues than at the temple worship in Jerusalem. Thus we feel no surprise when we see, perhaps more clearly in the Greek than even in Moffatt's translation, that St Peter had assumed a new post of responsibility for these Christians in Judaea. His visit to Samaria, so apparently St Luke wants us to understand, had branched out into a more general task of Church visitor, travelling ambassador of the mother Church at Jerusalem, performing miracles of healing, and even raising the dead Tabitha (Acts 9:32–42).

Was there any special reason why St Luke recorded St Peter's greatest miracle, the raising of Tabitha, just at this juncture? We have seen that his history of the early Church is an analytical, not a chronological one; we are therefore entitled to ask such a question. One thing may be said in advance. The miracle provided proof incontrovertible that God's Spirit was with St Peter also at the fateful decision which he was to take with regard to the centurion Cornelius, who, according to St Luke, was the first Gentile to be admitted into the Church of Christ. It might have been held that Cornelius was admitted by St Peter in a similar way to that in which he forced the completion of the Twelve or ordained the Seven, with a kind of bravado; but the miracles which he worked before are meant to prove that he had authority from God for this step, a step which incidentally was going to be questioned by St James and his adherents.

As for Cornelius, we know very little about him, as about most of these military men in Palestine. There are various reports in the Gospels dealing with officers from the Roman army. We have the report about the centurion at Capernaum whose servant was ill (Luke 7:2 ff. = Matt. 8:5 ff.). What may have become of him, we know not, neither is it more than a surmise that he was a recruiting officer: Jewish soldiers were frowned upon in the imperial army. There is also the centurion who stood on guard under the cross of Jesus and confessed, 'This man was certainly a (the) Son of God' (Mark 15:39); and finally we have the centurion Cornelius at Caesarea. They cannot be identified. It is possible that Cornelius would have been assigned the guard duty at the cross, but we have to realize that it was several years after the crucifixion that he was converted. The wisest thing to do is to take them as separate individuals when we ask, what was the power which made him 'constantly pray to God' (Acts 10:2).

An important find of the last twenty-five years, not very widely advertised, has shed much light upon the religion of the Roman army. We have now a so-called *feriale*, a list of feast days, for the Roman army, which was found at Dura-Europus on the river Euphrates, and published in 1940.[1] This *feriale* records the official religious practice of the particular auxiliary of the Roman army which was stationed at that outpost of the Roman Empire in A.D. 225–227, but which in broad outline is identical with similar calendars of feast days throughout the Roman army before and afterwards, the existence of which had been deduced by scholars for the last sixty years. It lists three groups of feast days: imperial feast days; feast days of the gods, especially the god of war, Mars, and his companion, Victory, the goddess of Rome; the goddess of the hearth-fire, Vesta; Neptune, the god of the sea, and Saturn, the god of agriculture; and finally military feast days, the days on which the veterans were dismissed and the days on which the field signs were garlanded. We see from this calendar that the Roman army kept its Church parades with the same punctiliousness and drabness as any other army. For these events were so common-place that no serious historian of the time ever wasted a word on them. Had it not been for this chance find, we might never have had any certainty about the whole business.

The spiritual hunger of the men who had to serve up to twenty-four years in the army, especially among these centurions, who were officers risen from the ranks, could not be satisfied with such meagre fare. Consequently there were numerous private cults springing up amongst the soldiery. From the second century onwards the cult of Mithras seems to have become the most popular in the army, but conversions to Christianity did also occur. Hippolytus of Rome made special provision for such cases in his *Church Order* of the beginning of the third century. They were regarded with somewhat mixed feelings by the ordinary Christians because they always brought with them the danger of persecution and martyrdom, not only for the new convert but also for the church into which he had been received.

[1] R. O. Fink, A. S. Hoey, W. F. Snyder, 'The *Feriale Duranum*', *Yale Classical Studies* 7 (1940), pp. 1 ff.

This psychological factor is of great importance for the understanding of St Luke's report of the conversion of the centurion Cornelius. For the present tendency of discarding the historicity of the events recorded in Acts compels us to stress time and again the intrinsic probability of these events, especially when we attempt to find out about those facts which Luke only hinted at, but did not fully disclose. However, there is another, typological aspect too, under which the conversion of Cornelius has to be judged. St Luke, as we have seen, made a critical selection of the events which he embodied in his history of the early days of the Church of Christ; and the fact that he made a Roman centurion the first Gentile convert to Christianity has its special significance. St Paul was the creator of the idea of 'the Church militant here in earth'. These various centurions who worship Christ are, therefore, introduced as soldiers of the greatest ruler on earth, the Roman Emperor, who bow to the might of the heavenly king.

The typological aspect of the story also comes out when we give some consideration to its placing in St Luke's narrative. In Acts 9:22 f., at the end of the story of Saul's conversion, which we have omitted so far, St Paul is represented as starting his ministry by preaching to the Jews. He did do so, according to Acts 9:29 f., even to the Jews at Jerusalem. In contrast to this it is St Peter who baptized the first Gentile. The implications of this most surprising change of place deserve a much fuller consideration than we have time to give to them. We would only mention the fact that already in the early Church the discrepancy in St Luke's report that it was St Peter who baptized the first Gentile, and St Paul's complaint about his vacillations at Antioch (Gal. 2:11 ff.) caused a certain amount of argument. This matter will come up in our next lecture.

Finally it has to be said that the story about the baptism of Cornelius shows features of a very considerable amount of polishing, which it seems to have received at the hands of St Luke. Once more the parallel between its construction and that of the report of St Paul's conversion (Acts 9:1 ff.) calls for attention. It is, to say the least, no common accident that the two visions of Ananias and Saul (Acts 9:10 ff.) should find their analogy in the two corresponding visions of Cornelius and St Peter. If only one double vision had been reported by St Luke, it would mean comparatively little; but here it is so obviously intended to draw our attention to the similarity between the blinded Saul on the one hand, who 'is praying at this very moment' (Acts 9:11), and Cornelius on the other, 'who constantly prayed to God' (Acts 10:2), that we must take notice of it. For the same similarity exists also between the refusal of Ananias (Acts 9:13),

'But, Lord', Ananias answered, 'many people have told me about all the mischief this man has done to thy saints at Jerusalem! . . .',

and St Peter's refusal (Acts 10:14):

No, no, my Lord; I have never eaten anything common or unclean.

Finally, the kindly and yet categorical reply of the divine voice to Ananias (Acts 9:15),

Go; I have chosen him to be the means of bringing my Name before the Gentiles and their kings as well as before the sons of Israel,

is, as it were, completed by the words heard by St Peter (Acts 10:15):

What God has cleansed, you must not count as common.

We are here in front of a great literary effort on the part of St Luke, and we are fortunate in that we are able to point to the literary model upon which this effort was based. It is the calling of the prophets of the Old Covenant which was re-enacted here by St Luke. Just as Samuel was called three times by the Lord (I Sam. 3), so St Peter was shown his vision three times (Acts 10:16); and just as various prophets remonstrated at their calling, so did Ananias and St Peter. It may even be held that God's promise about St Paul is a replica of the Song of the Suffering Servant (Isa. 42:1):

I have endowed him with my spirit, to carry true religion to the nations.

There are also numerous prophecies that the Gentiles will praise God's sacred name (Exod. 9:16; I Kings 8:43; I Chron. 22: 5; Ps. 86:9; Isa. 56:6, 62:2; Amos 9:12; Mal. 1:11, 14). In short, the Old Testament ring of this prophecy is unmistakable. Moreover, St Luke used the pattern of the initial unbelief of the chosen instrument of God in other connections too. The hesitation of Zechariah at the annunciation of the birth of John the Baptist comes to mind at once (Luke 1:18 ff.). We are thus given an opportunity of judging the considerable literary art which was at St Luke's command, by comparing the various ways in which he moulded this pattern to serve his literary purpose. Although the general thought that God's ways are so much higher than men's understanding is the same, the scenes which are chosen for exemplifying it are highly individual and appropriate to their purpose.

Comparing the vision of St Peter with the famous complaint of St Paul in Gal. 2:11 ff., we have to admit that the circumstances are very different indeed. First, the clash between the two apostles took place far from Palestine, at Antioch; secondly, it is stated in Gal. 2:12:

Before certain emissaries of James arrived, he ate along with the Gentile Christians; but when they arrived, he began to draw back and hold aloof, because he was afraid of the circumcision party.

At Jaffa, on the other hand, St Peter had boasted (Acts 10:14):

I have never eaten anything common or unclean.

Nevertheless, the divine command, 'what God has cleansed, you must not count as common' (Acts 10:15), was maintained by St Paul at Antioch with the same vigour as it was by the voice which St Peter had heard at Jaffa. Is it then at all thinkable that St Peter could have acted at Antioch as he did, if the incident of the conversion of Cornelius the centurion had happened to him, if the divine voice had preceded St Paul's shrill rebuke, and if he himself had prevailed upon the Church at Jerusalem that it must receive the first Gentile convert? Would it not, for instance, help considerably if it were to be assumed, as so many scholars do, that Cornelius became a full Jewish proselyte and was circumcised? We feel that the answers to these questions will vary greatly according to whether they are put in the abstract or with a conscious reference to the characters of the two men mentioned by St Paul, St Peter and St James of Jerusalem.

III

It is, therefore, necessary to analyse the defence of St Peter at Jerusalem (Acts 11:4 ff.) before we discuss the miracle at the house of Cornelius at Caesarea. In order to understand why St Peter was asked to defend himself, we have to refer once more to St Paul. He gives a very interesting piece of information about the matter in Gal. 6:12:

These men who are keen upon your getting circumcised are simply men who want to make a grand display in the flesh—it is only to avoid being persecuted for the cross of Christ.

'It was not against bigotry alone that St Paul had to contend', says Bishop Lightfoot in his commentary; 'his opponents were selfish and worldly also; they could not face the obloquy to which their abandonment of the Mosaic ordinances would expose them; they were not bold enough to defy the prejudices of their unconverted fellow-countrymen. And so they attempted to keep on good terms with them by imposing circumcision on the Gentile converts also, and thus getting the credit of zeal for the law. Even the profession of Jesus as Messiah by the Christians was a less formidable obstacle to their intercourse with the Jews than their abandonment of the law.'[1]

This statement puts the whole case for 'the circumcision party' (Acts 11:2) in a nutshell. They were afraid for their life at Jerusalem. St Stephen had been martyred on the accusation, 'we have heard him talking blasphemy against Moses and God' (Acts 6:11); St Philip had had to quit Jerusalem for the comparative safety of Caesarea because he had baptized first the Samaritans and then the eunuch of queen Candace; now St Peter had gone further still and received into the Church Cornelius who, as a Roman soldier, was legally as well as practically prevented from observing the Law, whether he was circumcised or not. He had to eat, sleep, live with his fellow-soldiers; the prescriptions about ritual purity, the rules about hours of prayer had simply no meaning for him, and moreover, he was a member of that most hated force which, from the fortress of Antonia, kept Jerusalem under its heel, the Italian cohort. Can we wonder at the fact that the Jerusalem Christians should rise up in arms? No, but how could they ever demand that St Peter, the prince of the apostles, should give an account of his action to them?

To answer this question let us hear the description which the Judaeo-Christian Hegesippus gave of St James of Jerusalem, as preserved in Eusebius's *Ecclesiastical History* (ii. 23:5 f.):

This man was holy from his mother's womb. He drank neither wine nor mead, nor did he eat meat. No scissors touched his head neither did he anoint his body with oil, or ever use a bath. He alone had the right of entering the holy place. He also wore no wool, but linen. He alone entered the temple and there he was found on his knees praying for the forgiveness of sins for the people, so that his knees were dried up like those of a camel, because he constantly bowed his knees and lay on them making intercession on behalf of the people.

That is, of course, legendary exaggeration; but we have also the testimony of Josephus (Ant. xx. 9:1, 201) about the martyrdom of James, which shows the respect he enjoyed amongst the Pharisees:

Since Ananos was that kind of man, he believed he had a chance when Festus had died and Albinus (his successor) was still on his way; and so he assembled the Sanhedrin for judgment and arraigned before it the brother of Jesus the

---

[1] J. B. Lightfoot, *Saint Paul's Epistle to the Galatians* (London, 1865), p. 222.

so-called Christ, James by name, and some others accused of breaking the Law, and handed them over for stoning. But those who were regarded as the most righteous and the most concerned about the Law in the city felt sore about this. They sent secretly to the Emperor, asking him to prevent Ananos from doing so, for he had no right to do so in the first place.

Ananos, Josephus goes on to inform us, was deprived of the high priesthood on account of his rash act.

Here then we have the portrait of a man whose sincerity could never be doubted, whose actions were as clearly defined as his standards were high, and who gained the deepest respect of the Gamaliels of this world, although they did not share his belief, but, if that criticism be allowed which, after all, is St Paul's criticism, who made the cross of Christ of no avail. He came as near as anybody to the standards of asceticism achieved by John the Baptist, of whom Jesus himself had said that 'no one has arisen among the sons of women who is greater than John the Baptist; and yet the least in the Realm of heaven is greater than he is' (Matt. 11:11). It was not St James himself who, even according to St Paul, took action in this controversy; but it was his hangers-on, his hero-worshippers, who took St Peter to task. Nevertheless St Peter, burdened with the memory of his denial of Jesus, which made him all the more despondent now, since he had been so hard on Simon Magus, gave an account of his baptizing Cornelius, and thus won the day by his humiliation. He gained nothing for himself by doing so. As a matter of fact, the eleventh chapter of Acts is not only the curtain-raiser for St Paul's mission to the Gentiles, but also for St Peter's flight from Jerusalem and the termination of the period of the Twelve by the execution of St James the Zebedaean.

IV

Once more we have to ask ourselves what the material was on which St Luke based his report of the baptism of Cornelius. Did he compose the speech of St Peter (Acts 11:5 ff.) out of the story in Acts 10, or did he spin the story out of the speech, or did he have both and only retailed them as he had received them? So far we have always found reasons to believe that any sermon which St Luke retailed was in existence before St Luke composed Acts, but in this case the balance is, if anything, against such an assumption. For the sermon leaves out the one salient point of the story—that the man who sent for St Peter (Acts 11:12) was the centurion Cornelius of the Italian cohort. Thus we conclude that the sermon of St Peter in Acts 11:5 ff. is no more than a rehash of the report of the conversion of Cornelius, as it was previously told in chapter 10, and was to be referred to once more by St Peter at the so-called council of the apostles (Acts 15:7). We shall therefore have to interpret the story told us in Acts 9:43 ff. in order to find out what St Luke's intentions were when he included it in Acts.

The first thing to notice is the care which St Luke has given to lending local colour to this story. Why, one might ask for instance, did he mention the house where St Peter stayed at Jaffa? What could 'Simon the tanner', who is mentioned three times (Acts 9:43; 10:6, 17) mean to Theophilus to whom Acts is dedicated? The answer can only be that St Luke wanted to give the name of a witness to the truth of his story. There is furthermore the description of the men whom Cornelius sent to fetch St Peter, two slaves and 'a religiously minded soldier' (Acts 10:7), whom St Peter received as guests and accompanied with a whole deputation of Christians from Jaffa. There is also the remark about St Peter being on 'the roof of the house about noon to pray' (Acts 10:9). That is a strange feature, since noon-time was not a time for public prayer, and praying on the roof was not common either. It is difficult to say whether anything more than local colour may be involved in this detail.

If these features make for a very realistic appearance of St Luke's report, there are yet others which have a typical significance. There is first of all the description of Cornelius as 'a religious man, who reverenced God with all his household and was liberal in his alms to the people, and who constantly prayed to God' (Acts 10:2). Cornelius was thus as nearly a Jew as he could be; and that did not only diminish the risk run by St Peter in receiving him into the Church, but also showed that the way to the Church went through the appreciation of the Old Testament. It is a feature of all St Paul's missionary work among the Gentiles, according to St Luke, that he addressed himself first to the Jews, the proselytes and the Gentile 'God-fearers'; and since the case of Cornelius was, so to speak, a test case for the mission to the Gentiles, this feature had to be included. The other feature of a more general significance is to be found in the meeting between Cornelius and St Peter, when Cornelius fell at St Peter's feet (Acts 10:25). At Rome at that very time the proud Romans resisted the demand of their crazy Emperor Caligula to worship him as a god. Here Cornelius, the worshipper of the most high God, is said to have fallen on his face before St Peter, and had to be reminded that the apostle too was 'only a man himself' (Acts 10:26), although he carried to

Cornelius the true message of salvation. The Roman Emperor was customarily described by the Greeks as 'the Saviour', and it seems that the tilt at him was intended by St Luke.

In contrast to this the story of the actual conversion of Cornelius is much more halting. The question asked by St Peter is awkwardly fashioned by St Luke. The reference to his vision (Acts 10:28) may yet pass muster, although it does not add anything to what we have been told already, for Cornelius and his friends (Acts 10:24b, where Moffatt's transposition makes indeed for an easier running of the narrative) did not know about it; but the apostle's question, 'Now I want to know why you sent for me?' (10:29) and the long-drawn reply of Cornelius (10:30–33) are not only cumbersome but preposterous. St Peter had heard all this from the envoys of Cornelius (Acts 10:22). These verses are the typical introduction for St Peter's sermon which is to follow (Acts 10:34–43), and this sermon is once more only thinly connected with the story. Here, I believe, we have a piece of the material on which St Luke did work, a missionary sermon applicable to almost any situation where the audience was well versed in the Old Testament. Only the reference to Acts 1:8, 'you will be my witnesses at Jerusalem, throughout all Judaea and Samaria and to the end of the earth', in Acts 10:42, shows the special purpose of the address—and it does anything but stress it since it only speaks of the witness 'to the People', i.e. to the Jews.

Thus the sermon of St Peter appears to us as striking the wrong note entirely. That becomes also quite clear when in the course of it 'the Holy Spirit fell upon all who listened to what he said' (Acts 10:44). This discord was also intended by St Luke, for he added the remark that 'the Jewish believers who had accompanied Peter were amazed that the gift of the Holy Spirit had been poured out on the Gentiles' (10:45). St Peter too was proved wrong, for these Gentiles had not even been baptized 'in the name of Jesus', like the Samaritans, nor had they received any laying on of hands. 'And he ordered them to be baptized in the name of Jesus Christ' (10:48). We cannot help suspecting a slight irony in these words of St Luke, for it seems unlikely that he should have forgotten already his remark in Acts 8:16. We would rather assume that he used these words in order to underline a certain lack of stability in the character of St Peter who, as also in the Gospel (for instance after his confession at Caesarea Philippi, Matt. 16:16), fell back far behind the recognition which he had already achieved. Thus we conclude that the baptism of Cornelius, St Peter being the man he was, is almost demanded as an explanation for his failure in his encounter with St Paul at Antioch.

6　The Church at Antioch

Drawing, it has been said, is the art of omitting the unnecessary. Thus St Luke has dealt only very briefly with the Church at Antioch which, along with Alexandria, was to become the most important Christian centre in the East. One of the reasons why it seems to us inadvisable to assign a late date to the book of Acts is just this treatment of the Antiochene Church. For already before the end of the first century Antioch had obtained a leading position in the Eastern Church, and established a firm understanding with the Church at Rome, which would have justified a more detailed exposition of its origins, if St Luke intended to give an account of them at all. Such an account, however, was demanded of him, since the Church at Antioch had played such a conspicuous part in the life of his hero St Paul.

St Luke has indeed made it quite evident that he dealt with the early history of the Church at Antioch for this very reason, by inserting the record of its earliest history immediately after his report of the baptism of the centurion Cornelius. If it is true that it was St Peter who in the course of his visitation of the Church in Judaea baptized the first Gentile convert—and we have seen that St Luke's narrative employed all the means at his disposal to convince us of this fact, as naming a witness (Simon the tanner), giving local colour to the story, referring to St Peter's rather unusual hour of prayer on the roof of the house, and stressing the typical significance of the event—it was nevertheless St Paul who was to become the apostle of the Gentiles, and who was now to carry out God's plan which had been revealed in St Peter's vision.

St Luke was in this instance faced with an extremely difficult literary task. He had to telescope a period of an unknown length, but which certainly, if we accept St Paul's account of it, extended over a number of years, of which at best he possessed only very scanty information, in order to make his narrative coherent. This is what St Paul recorded in Gal. 1:16 ff:

and when he chose to reveal his Son to me, that I might preach him to the Gentiles, instead of consulting with any human being, instead of going up to

Jerusalem to see those who had been apostles before me, I went off at once to Arabia, and on my return I came back to Damascus.

Then, after three years, I went up to Jerusalem to make the acquaintance of Cephas. I stayed a fortnight with him. I saw no other apostle, only James the brother of the Lord. (I am writing you the sheer truth, I swear it before God!) Then I went to the districts of Syria and Cilicia.

Thus St Paul's time-table, before St Barnabas came to call him from his home city of Tarsus to Antioch, would look as follows:

   i. Conversion at Damascus ('I came back to Damascus', Gal. 1:17).
   ii. Journey to 'Arabia', of an uncertain length.
   iii. Escape from Damascus (II Cor. 11:32 f.; 'after three years', Gal. 1:18).
   iv. Journey to Jerusalem, staying with St Peter for a fortnight (Gal. 1:18 f.).
   v. Living and journeying in 'the districts of Syria and Cilicia' (Gal. 1:21).

St Luke's account of these events in Acts 9:22 ff. leaves out the journey to Arabia as well as the return to Damascus, changes the account of St Paul's escape (Acts 9: 24, 25), in that it mentions the enraged Jews as his adversaries rather than King Aretas, and adds to St Paul's experiences at Jerusalem the preaching to the Hellenists and their adverse reaction. He also mentions that it was St Barnabas who introduced St Paul to the apostles.

We feel that these differences are by no means of a fundamental character. If St Paul's account is richer by the journey to Arabia which, because it does not appear to have been a missionary journey, is omitted by St Luke, it cannot be held that it contradicts St Luke's report. That is especially true with regard to St Paul's assurance that he was unknown 'to the Christian churches of Judaea' (Gal. 1:22). For this statement obviously aims only at the churches outside Jerusalem. At Jerusalem St Paul must have been known to numbers of Christians from his activities as a persecutor of the Church. Therefore no exception should be taken to the report of St Paul's preaching to the Hellenists at Jerusalem and the reason for his premature departure. Only the fact that he does not mention the part played by St Barnabas in introducing him to St Peter may make us wonder, and here we feel that it may have been the later disagreement between them which made for St Paul's suppression of this incident. It is, of course, equally possible that it just slipped his mind.

So much for the early years of St Paul's career as a Christian. There followed several years in Syria and Cilicia (Gal. 1:21), during which his missionary activities seem to have touched no more than a comparatively small circle around his home at Tarsus in Cilicia. The reason for his retirement to Tarsus for such a long period we do not know. Neither he nor St Luke gives any indication as to whether or not the two apostles whom he had met at Jerusalem, St Peter and St James of Jerusalem, were in disagreement with him. There is the statement in Gal. 1:17 about 'those who had been apostles before me', which indicates that already at that time St Paul claimed to be an apostle of Jesus Christ, and stated this claim on his first visit to Jerusalem. This, coming as it did from a former persecutor of the Church, must have been a tremendous shock to the two. The strength of character which was needed by them to accept St Paul not just as a Christian, but as a fellow-apostle, was indeed of the highest order. For he was obviously an intruder in the circle of the apostles, as he himself admits in I Cor. 15:8 f., and the words in Acts 9:29 f.,

when the brothers learned that the Hellenists were attempting to make away with him, they took him down to Caesarea and sent him off to Tarsus,

seem to breathe a feeling of relief on the part of the Jerusalem Church. It may be conjectured that St Paul met that other firebrand, St Philip, at Caesarea, when he passed through there. We have, however, no means to check this conjecture, for Caesarea was the obvious port for a departure by sea from Jerusalem. However, considering everything, it is undeniable that St Philip, if he was then already stationary at Caesarea, must have been interested in meeting a man who had so narrowly escaped suffering the same fate as had overtaken his friend St Stephen.

II

Our Lord's words in Matt. 11:12,

From the days of John the Baptist until now, they are pressing into the Realm of heaven—these eager souls are storming it!

which Luke 16:16 has preserved as

The Law and the prophets lasted till John; since then the good news of the Realm of God is preached, and anyone presses in,

might have been written as a record of the events which were taking place during the time that St Paul was living in a semi-retirement at Tarsus, occupied we know not how. The growth of the Church in Jerusalem, Judaea and Samaria, summed up in Acts 9:31 ff., was an idyll when compared to the spreading of the gospel abroad. Cadbury[1] has very properly referred to the surprising remark of the Roman historian Suetonius[2] that at Rome under the rule of the Emperor Claudius, some time between A.D. 41 and 54, major Jewish riots occurred *impulsore Chresto*, caused by Chrestus, who may be, and probably is no other than, Jesus Christ; and also to the difficult interpretation of the ambiguously worded letter sent by the same Emperor in A.D. 41 to Alexandria[3] which has caused, to say the least, a very real suspicion that Christian preaching had made itself felt there too. We have good reasons to believe that St Paul's Epistle to the Romans was conceived in A.D. 55, and that at that time the Church at Rome was already fully established— we do not know by whom. Only one thing seems to be certain, that it cannot have been St Peter, unless we jettison the whole evidence contained about him in Acts.

The historical description of this worldwide expansion of the Christian Church at this early date was still more complicated by the very varying and frequently very unorthodox ways in which the gospel of Christ seems to have been represented and often—no doubt—misrepresented by these early missioners. In order to substantiate this fact we have to consider first that, on the one hand, these men had as yet no authoritative, written record of the life and work, the death and resurrection of Jesus Christ, on which they might have based their addresses, and that on the other the Church actively encouraged and supported prophecy and speaking in tongues. We just cannot imagine the diversity of the Christian message when it was spread abroad in this way. It is at least unknown whether any other of these early missionaries took the same precautions as St Paul by going, if only after three years of active missionary work, to meet St Peter in order to obtain such instructions as he was willing and able to give, or whether, having been baptized 'in the Name of the Lord Jesus', and thus being endowed with the gift of the Holy Spirit, they felt sufficiently qualified to preach the gospel forthwith, and to found churches without any further information. The great miracle at the early spreading of the Christian mission was not that the message of salvation went out so quickly, but that the unity in the Holy Spirit was

---

[1] H. J. Cadbury, *The Book of Acts in History* (New York, 1955), pp. 115 f.
[2] *Life of Claudius*, 25:4.
[3] H. I. Bell, *Jews and Christians in Egypt* (London, 1924), pp. 1 ff.

at all preserved and the identity of the message was still recognizable, in spite of the fact that no written record of Jesus Christ was in existence and no recital of a creed was demanded for holy baptism.

Practically all that St Luke has done in order to enlighten us on this development is this: that, on the one hand, he gives us an impression of the high importance which was accorded to the mother Church at Jerusalem in these stormy years, and on the other briefly outlines the events in one of those new churches, the Church at Antioch. In that way he has made it very difficult for us to find out any details about the progress of the gospel all over the world, before St Paul came on the scene. One of the greatest Church historians who ever lived, Adolf Harnack, has stated in all sincerity that the early Church could claim no more than two missioners, one very great, St Paul, and, on a moderate scale, St Peter.[1] That accords well with the widespread impression that in those years between A.D. 37 and 42/3 the apostles were enjoying a time of leisure at Jerusalem, and—is all moonshine. Behind St Luke's words (Acts 9:31), 'the Church . . . increased in numbers', there lies a record of very hard work when the apostles were probably overrun with problems of heresy and orthodoxy, executing their power of 'binding and unbinding', and where the two sayings of the Lord, 'he who is not against us is for us', and 'he who is not with me is against me, and he who does not gather with me scatters', had to be balanced carefully in all the cases of suspected erroneous doctrine. All that we can do in order to understand this situation is to use our historical imagination when we read in Acts 8:14,

When the apostles at Jerusalem heard that Samaria had accepted the word of God,

and again in Acts 11:22,

News of this reached the church in Jerusalem.

We are entitled to do so because the writing of history was at that time very largely confined to the writing of the history of the leading men, historical biography, as one might call it. The history of composite bodies, like the Church, was still in its infancy. St Luke in particular was given to this writing of a history of the apostles rather than of the apostolic Church. We are, therefore, entitled to use our historical imagination in order to draw conclusions from the individual event to

[1] A. Harnack, *The Acts of the Apostles*, E. T. (London, 1909), pp. xix ff., 117 ff.

general conditions. Such are the general preliminaries for the appreciation of that very short, and at the same time most important passage:
Acts 11:19–30.

III

In this passage every word is full of meaning. The story begins once
more with a reference to the martyrdom of St Stephen. That is to make
us realize that it goes right back behind the confirmation of the Samaritans, the conversion of St Paul, and the baptism of the centurion
Cornelius. We have stressed the fact repeatedly, but cannot stress it
enough, that St Luke's account of the history of the early Church is not
a chronological, but an analytical one. This passage is one of the most
important examples for this thesis of ours. All through the first half of
Acts the events in the inner circle of the Church are given priority by St
Luke over those at the periphery. The shift of balance from the Jewish
to the Gentile Church is only setting in in the course of the tenth and
eleventh chapters of Acts. The centre of the Church, we are to understand, lies still at Jerusalem. This fact is brought out most clearly in that
St Luke does not mention any names of the fugitives from Jerusalem who
came to Antioch. It is, of course, possible that he did not know who they
were; but on the whole that seems not to be a very inviting hypothesis.
First of all he mentions that there were Cypriotes and Cyrenians among
them, and secondly we can put our finger to both a Cypriote and a
Cyrenian whom he must have known, and from whom he might have
had the information about these men. The Cypriote is, of course, St
Barnabas, and the Cyrenian is Simon of Cyrene, the father of Alexander
and Rufus (Mark 15:21). The assumption that St Luke did not know
them can more or less be ruled out, not only for St Barnabas but also for
Rufus, whose name appears once more in Rom. 16:13: 'Salute that choice
Christian, Rufus.' The identification is probable, and the conclusion is at
hand that he was an acquaintance of St Paul, and probably of St Luke
also.

It is, therefore, a precarious assumption that St Luke did not know the
founders of the Church at Antioch, and all the more precarious to deduce
from it that the old tradition cannot be true that St Luke himself was a
native of Antioch. We would rather suggest that he had an exceptionally
good knowledge of conditions and personalities, but found that there
was not one of sufficient stature amongst these early preachers, who had

come to Antioch, to be singled out for being mentioned by name. Indeed these men were a curious crowd, as may be seen from the only genuine reference to early Christian mission work outside the Acts of the Apostles, which has come down to us in Eusebius, *Ecclesiastical History* (iii. 37:1–3):

And, in addition to these, others too became known as the first generation of Christians after the apostles. These men, being the worthy pupils of such teachers, built upon the foundations for churches which the apostles had laid throughout the whole world, augmenting greatly the preaching of the message of salvation, and sowing the saving seeds of the kingdom of heaven through all the length and breadth of the civilized world. For most of the disciples of that time, who for love of philosophy gave their life to the Divine Logos, first obeyed the divine command to distribute their whole fortune for the relief of others and then, being sent abroad, to follow the vocation of evangelists, and to count it their gain to preach to those who so far had not heard at all the word of faith, the Christ, and to hand to them the holy Gospels in writing. They themselves did no more than to lay the foundations of the faith in foreign places, and to establish others as shepherds, entrusting them with the cure of the newly gathered-in Christians, but went forth to other districts and tribes with the grace and help of God . . .

This report which, as we believe, was taken from the *Apology* of an early Christian apologist, Quadratus, gives you a picture of these earliest Christian missionaries, very similar to the itinerant apostles of socialism at the end of the last and the beginning of this century. These men were only loosely attached to the Jerusalem apostles and did as the Spirit bade them. Quite unaware of the implications of their activities, they started preaching the gospel to the Gentiles, leaving it to the apostles to regularize what they had done. Throughout Phoenicia and Cyprus, we are told, they limited their efforts to the missionarizing of the Jews; but once they had reached Antioch, they addressed the 'Greeks' also. Most surprisingly St Luke adds (Acts 11:21):

the strong hand of the Lord was with them, and a large number believed and turned to the Lord.

For, indeed, a new situation was arising which had not been foreseen: the 'middle wall of partition' between Jews and Gentiles had collapsed. What had started at Jerusalem as a Jewish sect, closely akin in many respects to the Pharisaic order, the Church, suddenly had to make provision for followers who had proved immune from Jewish proselytizing, and even now wanted to have nothing in common with the Jews, but accepted the curiously Latin sounding name of Christians (Acts 11:26).

It is understandable that the Church at Jerusalem viewed these develop-
ments with alarm. What is surprising is the choice of the envoy who
was to regularize the position at Antioch (Acts 11:22):

News of this reached the church in Jerusalem, and they despatched Barnabas to
Antioch.

For St Barnabas was not one of the Twelve. We can understand, perhaps,
why it was not St Peter who was sent, because he had been put in charge
of the churches in Judaea. However, there were others, St John or his
brother St James, for instance, men who must have been in considerable
danger at that time in Jerusalem, as we see from the short notice about
the martyrdom of St James (Acts 12:1 f.):

It was about that time that king Herod laid hands of violence on some members
of the church. James the brother of John he slew with the sword.

It would, therefore have seemed expedient for the mother Church to
send one of them to the comparative safety of Antioch. The fact that it
was a place of comparative safety appears clearly, when we combine the
report of St Peter's escape from Jerusalem (Acts 12:17 fin.), 'and off he
went to another place', with St Paul's remark (Gal. 2:11), 'when Peter
came to Antioch', as it is customarily done.

However, it is to the great credit of the Jerusalem Church that such
considerations, if they existed, played no part in its ultimate decision.
It was the 'Levite of Cypriote birth' (Acts 4:36), St Barnabas, who was
to represent the mother Church at Antioch, obviously because of the
'Cypriotes and Cyrenians' (Acts 11:20) who had begun missionarizing
the Gentiles. One thought comes to mind at once, that St Luke omitted
this vital information here, because the nationality of St Barnabas must
have been common-place with his readers, a small point in favour of an
early date of Acts. But that is only to emphasize the importance of the
mission of St Barnabas. He was sent to Antioch as a person who was
well aware of the personalities and circumstances involved. However,
the question which seems to us decisive is that of the brief he held. What
was the authority of the Church at Jerusalem to take action in this matter?

IV

For we are here faced with the fact that the Church at Jerusalem—and
not the apostles—provided for a sort of supervision or inspection of

69

another Church of Christ, which it could not on any account claim to form part of itself. The Church in Samaria was at any rate situated within the ancient kingdom of David, in the territory of the twelve tribes of Israel. The sending of St Peter and St John to Samaria must be understood in that light as a step towards the re-constitution of the kingdom of David. The mission of St Barnabas, on the other hand, envisaged Jesus Christ as the King of the whole world, with its universal capital at Jerusalem. To speak in terms of the time, St Barnabas appeared as the first legate of Christ the Emperor. That was also in St Luke's mind when he referred to the fact that St Barnabas took it upon himself to call in the help of St Paul. Normally Acts 11:25 f.—

So Barnabas went off to Tarsus to look for Saul, and on finding him he brought him to Antioch, where for a whole year they were guests of the church and taught considerable numbers—

is understood to mean that St Paul was then at a loose end at Tarsus, and was rescued from his obscurity for the work of Christ by St Barnabas. Now that may well have been so, but it is by no means the whole case. First of all, it does not seem to agree too well with St Paul's own statement (Gal. 1:22 f.), that

the Christian churches of Judaea . . . heard that 'our former persecutor is now preaching the faith he once harried', which made them praise God for me.

We are prepared to admit that St Paul's work at Tarsus was rather small fry, but there should be no doubt that he was acting at the head of a Church at Tarsus. One just cannot conceive of St Paul as laying off the work, for which he was divinely called, for several years. Neither are we at all happy about Moffatt's translation according to which St Barnabas and St Paul were 'guests' of the Church at Antioch for over a year. That is true only in the sense that they were outsiders, admitted by the Church of Antioch, but not fully established members. This recognition is important, for it sheds light on the remark about St Barnabas (Acts 11:24):

for he was a good man, full of the holy Spirit and faith.

We must not think that his authority was so self-evident that he could just take over the leadership of the Church at Antioch. If, as St Luke maintains (Acts 11:19), that Church had been founded by fugitives from Jerusalem, their feelings towards the apostles, who had remained at Jerusalem, cannot have been very friendly. This consideration brings us to realize the courage and wisdom that was required of St Barnabas when he decided to call Saul, one of the chief persecutors, to his assistance at Antioch. It was the spirit of forgiveness shown by him which won the day for him, and caused the Church at Antioch to become in later time one of the bulwarks of Judaistic Christianity. This observation brings us once more to the question of the authority of the Jerusalem Church, and we have to conclude that it rested first and foremost upon the person of St Barnabas, who won his way to the hearts of the first Church of the Gentiles. He succeeded in bringing the Church at Antioch to the acceptance of the Jerusalem point of view that there must be unity in the Church where the universal forgiveness of sins—even where transgression had been as blatant as in the person of the persecutor Saul —was administered. We can only add as a question, whether the Church at Jerusalem may have failed to find an equally successful ambassador to the Church at Alexandria? For if we accept Cadbury's interpretation of the letter of the Emperor Claudius to the Alexandrians,[1] we cannot doubt that such ambassadors were actually sent from Jerusalem to Alexandria.

The position of the Jerusalem Church was further strengthened at Antioch by the great disaster which befell the mother Church, together with the whole country of Palestine, in the year A.D. 47/8. That year was a sabbatical year, during which, according to Lev. 25:3 ff., the Jews had to leave their fields fallow, and therefore had to rely on the import of food from abroad. However, as the prophet Agabus had 'showed by the Spirit that a severe famine was about to visit the whole world' (Acts 11:28), the harvest of A.D. 47 proved exceptionally poor throughout Syria. There was no surplus to be exported to Palestine, and the whole population of Judaea, including the Christians, found themselves in a terrible predicament. In this situation the Church at Antioch rallied to accept its responsibility for 'the brothers in Judaea' (Acts 11:29) and sent 'their contribution to the presbyters by Barnabas and Saul' (Acts 11:30).

v

It is to be assumed that by the time this happened St Barnabas and St Paul were no longer hospitants only in the Church at Antioch. The persecution of the Church at Jerusalem had taken place in A.D. 34/5 as

[1] H. J. Cadbury, *The Book of Acts in History* (New York, 1955), pp. 116 f.

we have seen. Thus, at a conservative estimate, the Church at Antioch had begun to missionarize the Greeks in A.D. 39/40; St Barnabas must have gone there in A.D. 40/1, and St Paul must have joined him in A.D. 41/2. 'For a whole year', Acts 11:26 says, they were 'guests'[1] there; but it is evident from the context that they did not leave immediately after that one year, but were now at last fully accepted members. In A.D. 42/3 St Peter fled from Jerusalem, and the conflict between him and St Paul, as described in Gal. 2:11 ff., took place. St Luke is silent about this, and we are once more left to guess the final outcome of the conflict. It appears, however, that St Paul championed the popular opinion at Antioch, and that St Peter departed admitting defeat. However that may be, it is certain that he left whilst St Paul stayed at Antioch and was even chosen by the Antiochene Christians to take their contribution 'to the presbyters' at Jerusalem (Acts 11:30).

Here we are faced with two great questions. The one is, whether this is the journey to Jerusalem to which St Paul refers in Gal. 2:1 ff.:

> Then, fourteen years later, I went again to Jerusalem, accompanied by Barnabas; I took Titus with me also. (It was in consequence of a revelation that I went up at all.) I submitted the gospel I am in the habit of preaching to the Gentiles, submitting it privately to the authorities, to make sure that my course of action would be and had been sound.

In view of the definite date, A.D. 48, which is exactly fourteen years later than St Paul's conversion in A.D. 34/5, the conclusion has to be drawn that this is indeed the same incident as that mentioned in Acts 11:30. It follows from this that St Paul in Gal 2:11 ff. referred to an event which was considerably earlier than his second visit to Jerusalem. That is a small matter and does not, so we believe, detract from the reliability of his report. St Luke, on the other hand, left out the negotiations between St Barnabas, St Paul and Titus on the one hand and St James of Jerusalem, St Peter and St John on the other, just as St Paul omitted the ostensible purpose of their visit to Jerusalem, the handing over of the relief funds collected by the Church at Antioch, although it seems certain that the revelation, on account of which St Paul allegedly travelled to Jerusalem, had been no other than the prophecy of Agabus. St Paul would have weakened his case with the Galatians if there had been any suggestion that he and St Barnabas had arrived at Jerusalem with such a much needed gift as they actually brought. St Luke, on the other hand, reserved these negotiations for his dramatic description of the so-called council of

---

[1] An unsatisfactory rendering; see p. 70.

the apostles (Acts 15:1 ff.), and the question whether or not such a council ever took place will occupy our minds in the next lecture.

We have, however, to concern ourselves yet with the Jerusalem side of the picture. Our second question is, who were those 'presbyters' mentioned in Acts 11:30? Let us first give a preliminary answer: They were the same as 'the authorities' referred to in Gal. 2:6. For this term of St Paul's it has been suggested with good reason, that it was an equivalent to the rabbinical title of honour *chashub*, which was used to describe informally the elders of a synagogue. The distinction of the men to whom he referred was therefore a typically Jewish one. However, St Paul did not give them the title *zāqēn*, the title presupposed by St Luke, that given to the 'elders', members of the Jerusalem Sanhedrin. Here indeed we find a substantial disagreement between St Luke and St Paul. St Paul could write (Gal. 2:6):

it makes no difference to me what they were: God does not regard the outward appearance of men.[1]

St Luke, on the other hand, acknowledged their status as the Sanhedrin of the new Israel of God, not only here but also in Acts 15:2, 23, and again in Acts 21:18.

From this we can measure the growth of the influence of the Jerusalem Church, which indeed contrived to make the most of the success gained on her behalf by St Barnabas at Antioch. The extent of its authority was as yet undefined—and remained so because of the destruction of Jerusalem in A.D. 70; but during those twenty years from A.D. 48 to 68 there was a real chance that the Christian Sanhedrin at Jerusalem would claim an authority over the Christian churches abroad analogous to that exercised by the Jewish Sanhedrin over the synagogues of the dispersion. We can see traces of these efforts everywhere in the Pauline epistles, and we have to admit that St Paul was fighting a losing battle. The war between the established Church government and the inspired missioner and leader of the Church had begun. It continues to this day, and will do so to the end of the world.

However, St Luke's story has only reached this point in Acts 11:30. Not only Acts 12, which marks the end of the apostolic period of the Church at Jerusalem, and the fact that the Jerusalem presbyters were not necessarily identical with the apostles, by recording the martyrdom of St James and the imprisonment of St Peter, refers to an earlier time, as

[1] Moffatt imports a nuance probably unintended by Paul when he translates: 'it makes no difference to me what their status used to be . . .'

we have seen already, but also Acts 13–14, the report of the first missionary journey of St Barnabas and St Paul. Once again we have to stress the fact that St Luke strove for a logical arrangement of his story, and that he wanted to carry the history of the Church at Antioch to its completion, before he entered upon that of the Jerusalem Church once more, and then upon the missionary enterprises of St Paul and St Barnabas. We have also to remember that, although there was an universal calendar in the Roman Empire, computed according to the accession of Roman consuls on the 1st of January in each year, these years were not numbered consecutively, and people were not as calendar-minded then as we are now. Especially in the first century A.D. the Roman calendar was as yet a new importation into the eastern half of the Empire, and the length of his jumps forward and backward was probably not fully appreciated by St Luke. At any rate, Acts 12 has to be fixed in the years A.D. 42/3, and Acts 13–14 in the years A.D. 45–47.

Thus we should understand Acts 13:1 ff., in the light of Acts 11:27 ff., in the following way:

When the Church at Antioch, on the prophecy of Agabus that the Church at Jerusalem would soon be in need of material assistance, made preparations to meet this emergency, its leaders were Barnabas, Symeon called Niger, and Lucius the Cyrenian, besides Menahem, the foster-brother of Herod the tetrarch, and Saul. They were teachers and prophets themselves, like Agabus, fully in favour of the cause. However, to the greatest consternation of the people, the two most active ones were sent away as missioners at the command of the Holy Spirit. They had to leave their task to Menahem with his close connections with Jerusalem, and Lucius, the leader of those Cyrenians who had inaugurated the mission to the Greeks. These two opposites had to agree, the first to a further extension of the mission to the Gentiles, the second on helping the Jerusalem Church, which in time past had failed him. And thus was the work successfully accomplished.

7 Judaism, Christianity and the Empire

I

The book of Acts cannot be properly understood, if it is not seen within the political setting of its time. It is true that the political character of religion has at no time been entirely overlooked; but the religious character of politics has never been sufficiently appreciated. Yet our own time has witnessed as much as any other to the fundamental character of religion rather than politics. We ourselves have witnessed the rise of communist Russia in the years since 1917, and yet we are still unwilling to draw this obvious conclusion from it. We will claim that Lenin was a political genius, whereas, if genius at all, he was a philosophical genius; we will maintain that Stalin was a political master-mind, whereas he was in truth no more than a cunning mediocrity; and we will even set our best brains to analyse the political implications of their successors' words and actions; but we stubbornly refuse to see the obvious, namely that we are faced with a religious movement, comparable to the rise of Islam in the eighth century; and that the greatest force in politics is the religious devotion of the masses to some political vision.

Like Russia—and she has indeed inherited this conception from Rome by way of Byzantium—the Roman Empire was founded upon a religious conception. It was a sacred Empire, sponsored by the gods as an instrument for the salvation of mankind. It was meant to establish 'peace upon earth, goodwill towards mankind', for *pax*, peace, and *humanitas*, meaning both 'mankind' and 'goodwill towards mankind', were two of its greatest ideals, indeed perhaps its most popular watchwords in the East. With the help of a preposterously small army these aims of Roman imperial policy were achieved, because the Roman administration succeeded in inspiring its subject races with the religious idea of imperial universalism or cosmopolitanism. In order to grasp the meaning of this unique achievement we have to look at two facts only, the vanishing of the vernacular languages—in the East before the impact of the 'civilized' Greek language, and in the West before the ruling Latin language—and the assimilation of all the local deities with the gods of the Greek Olympus and the Roman Capitol. The effects of this 'theocrasy', mixture of deities, were so complete that the most painful and scrupulous efforts of modern scholarship to unscramble it have been, on the whole, unavailing. The 'religious historians' of today are still largely chasing fancies rather than finding solid facts. Incidentally, if any national religion would not or could not conform to the general imperial religion it was ruthlessly suppressed, like Druidism in Gaul and Britain.

The Roman attitude towards Judaism might have been just as ruthless, if the Jews had not learned the use of civilized means in the defence of their religion. The barbarous, Palestinian Zealots could be crushed, and met that fate at the hands of Pompey in 63 B.C., and again of Titus in A.D. 70, and of Hadrian in A.D. 135. However, the pleas for toleration put forward by the Pharisees, the representation of Judaism as a philosophy by men like Philo of Alexandria, the numerous forgeries of the first centuries before and after Christ by which the Jews of this period attempted to prove that their religion was actually the basis upon which Greek or at least Hellenistic philosophy had been erected, and above all the unreserved acceptance of the universalistic ideal, which transformed the earlier national religion of the Jews during the Hellenistic era, seemed to make it worth while for the Roman rulers to pay the price demanded by Judaism for its collaboration within the Empire, rather than to use violence against the Jews.

This price was indeed a heavy one. The visible symbol of the unity of the Roman Empire was the Roman Emperor. In the East, which already had a long tradition of ruler worship, he was accorded divine honours. Not only were there temples built for him—we know in particular of one in Syria which was dedicated to the Emperor Claudius, but we may also mention the fact that even in his life-time Augustus received a temple at Alexandria, originally intended for Mark Antony—and sacrifices offered before his statues, but all the various symbols of Roman imperial power, like the eagles of the legions, were given a religious meaning. The Jews objected to all this on the strength of the second commandment, and were therefore exempted from Emperor-worship as well as from military service, where these symbols played a conspicuous part. Moreover, the Jewish religious service amongst the Jews of the dispersion demanded an active participation of the faithful. It seems probable that in the course of time the mystery religions too formed similar groups of worshippers; but the ancient sanctuaries confined all the action in the divine services to the temple personnel. The worshippers were at best admitted to processions outside the temple buildings. A congregation of the faithful was not formed. The Roman government too had its serious misgivings concerning the formations of clubs, lodges

and all sorts of private societies, which were kept under strictest sur-
veillance and frequently closed by the police; but Jewish synagogues
were only rarely interfered with, and only in cases of real emergency.
Finally, and this was indeed the least significant concession to the Jews,
the temple enclosure at Jerusalem was barred by the Roman government
to all non-Jews, and the penalty for a contravention of this rule was
death.

It is understandable that these privileges granted to the Jews were of
the highest value to the enormous expansion of Judaism in the first one-
and-a-half centuries of the Roman Empire. If they caused a fierce
antagonism to the Jews amongst the heathen populace, they nevertheless
shielded them from the danger of persecution by the civil authorities.
Moreover, up to the fall of Jerusalem, these favours were granted
liberally to all who professed to be Jews, and made their Jewish profession known by the one incontrovertible proof offered by their religion,
circumcision. Heretical sects were numerous amongst the Jews of the
dispersion. The most learned inquiry into the life of the Jewish synagogues at Rome[1] (of which there were many) has cast doubt upon the
orthodoxy of all the Jews living at the imperial capital, if orthodoxy was
to be assessed by rabbinical standards. However, the Roman administration refused to apply any standards of orthodoxy, and the result of the
respective attitudes of the rulers and the people to the Jews of the
dispersion may be judged by the famous scene at Corinth, as described
in Acts 18:14 ff.:

Paul was just on the point of opening his lips to reply, when Gallio said to the
Jews, 'If it had been a misdemeanour or wicked crime, there would be some
reason in my listening to you, O Jews. But as these are merely questions of
words and persons and your own Law, you can attend to them for yourselves.
I decline to adjudicate upon matters like that.' And he drove them from the
tribunal. Then all the Greeks caught hold of Sosthenes the president of the
synagogue and beat him in front of the tribunal; but Gallio took no notice.

Here we have the whole case of Judaism in the Roman Empire in a
nutshell; their privileged status which made them approach imperial
dignitaries with very little reserve, the reluctance of even a man like
Gallio, the brother of Seneca (who, at that time, was not only the most
celebrated Roman philosopher, but was also soon to become the Prime
Minister of the Emperor Nero), to deal with their internal quarrels, and

---

[1] P. Rieger and H. Vogelstein, *Geschichte der Juden in Rom* (Berlin, 1896); cf.
H. J. Leon, *The Jews of Ancient Rome* (Philadelphia, 1960).

the open contempt for them on the part of the masses, who took whatever opportunity offered itself to use violence against them. Incidentally, it is to be assumed that the police force which was at Gallio's disposal would have proved insufficient to give protection to Sosthenes.

II

Christianity, as we have said in our previous lecture, had begun as a Jewish sect. Its adherents, even if they were suspect to the Jewish authorities at Jerusalem, could claim the privileges granted to the Jews, and it would have gone hard for the Jews to disown them so long as the Christians adopted the practice of circumcision and the Jewish food laws. That is the interpretation of St Paul's well-known complaint, (Phil. 3:18 f.):

For many—as I have often told you and tell you now with tears—many live as enemies of the cross of Christ. Destruction is their fate, the belly is their god [a reference to the Jewish food laws], they glory in their shame [a reference to the circumcision], these men of earthly mind! [a reference to the Jewish privileges].

However, this was the summing up of many years of struggle on the part of St Paul. When he was still at Antioch such an all-or-nothing attitude had not yet been reached by him. We have gathered from the story of the conversion of the centurion Cornelius that so far he had only preached the gospel to the Jews. Now, about A.D. 45, he was going to enter upon his new task, the preaching to the Gentiles, and for this he received his commissioning in the most formal manner.

St Luke has recorded the commissioning of St Paul and St Barnabas in Acts 13:2 f.:

As they were worshipping the Lord and fasting, the holy Spirit said, 'Come! set me apart Barnabas and Saul for the work to which I have called them.' Then after fasting and praying they laid their hands on them and let them go.

There was, therefore, no direction given to the two apostles as to what they should do, and it appears at first sight that the command of the Holy Spirit was, as we have said in our previous lecture, both unexpected and disturbing. It was a seemingly unspecified command: St Barnabas and St Paul, we are given to understand, were not needed in the work at Antioch any longer.

Two points remain to be cleared up before we go any further: the one personal, the other material. The personal point concerns John Mark who, according to Acts 12:25, had been brought up by the two from Jerusalem to Antioch on that journey which, as we concluded in our last lecture, only took place after the first missionary journey of St Barnabas and St Paul, but who, as we learn from Acts 13:13, 'left them and went back to Jerusalem', or, as it is put in Acts 15:38, 'had deserted them in Pamphylia'. This second verse suggests that he had left them there against their wish, certainly against St Paul's wish. The material is too scanty to allow of more than a hypothetical explanation. It appears, however, that Acts 12:25 is in an even greater textual disorder than one might expect. Moffatt's translation[1] certainly rests upon a minority reading, supported by 'D', which has the advantage of giving an understandable sense, but which should yet be rejected, because 'D' presupposes another context. The majority reading has, 'Barnabas and Saul returned to Jerusalem, having accomplished their ministry, taking with them John surnamed Mark.' For this we have, of course, no supporting evidence whatever; but it would fit in after Acts 15:2. Conversely, if we were to accept Moffatt's reading, we could fit in the verse after Acts 15:33, where there is a similar uncertainty—verse 34 finding only scanty support, as you may see from Moffatt, who omits it—and where a remark about the return of the two apostles to Antioch seems to have been left out. But in the place where it is now found Acts 12:25 is a misfit and should not be taken notice of. St Mark accompanied the apostles either on their journey to the apostles' council, or from that council back to Antioch.

The second point is the ceremony of the laying on of hands upon St Barnabas and St Paul. The ceremony has occurred twice already, in Acts 6:6, at the ordination of the Seven, and in Acts 8:17, at the confirmation of the Samaritans. Neither of these two cases forms a real precedent here. In view of the use of the technical term, 'separate me Barnabas and Saul' (Acts 13:2), which seems to repeat the command of Num. 8:14, 'thus shalt thou separate the Levites from among the children of Israel', we have come to the conclusion that this conception lay at the bottom of the ceremony here. If that be the case, we must ask in what sense the sending out of missioners could be compared with the 'separation of the Levites'. It is at least suggestive to point to the fact that the Levites had no territory amongst the tribes of Israel. If this idea be accepted, we can see why the two apostles without any further ado went

[1] 'After fulfilling their commission, Barnabas and Saul returned from Jerusalem, bringing with them John who is surnamed Mark.'

on their missionary journey. The laying on of hands meant that they were given the farewell by the Church at Antioch. Whilst Acts 13:1 shows them as established ministers in that Church, Acts 13:2, 3 'separates' them from this or any other permanently established Church, and throws new light also upon the report from Eusebius or Quadratus, which we read in our former lecture, on the early evangelists who, having rid themselves of their property, would never stay in any one place, but as soon as they had sown the seed of the gospel would repair to another. Thus Acts 13:2, 3 should be regarded as the *leitmotif* for all that St Luke has to say afterwards on St Paul's journeys. Here he became, to quote Sir William Ramsay, 'St Paul the traveller'.

III

Viewed from this angle, St Luke's abrupt beginning (Acts 13:4), 'sent out thus by the holy Spirit, they went down to Seleucia and from there they sailed to Cyprus', makes sense. These two men were let loose by the Holy Spirit upon the whole world; but their first destination was the harbour town of Antioch, and from there they went to the birthplace of St Barnabas, the island of Cyprus. There 'they proclaimed the word of God in the Jewish synagogues' (Acts 13:5). Thus it is made clear that St Paul even yet had not discovered his real vocation, which was the mission to the Gentiles, and the result was accordingly negligible. Neither Salamis nor Paphos became churches of Pauline foundation.

If we take Acts 13:6, 'they covered the whole island', at its face value, their work must have lasted quite a time, for there were fourteen townships in the island, and travelling by ship from one to the next, they must have spent at least four to five months in them, experiencing the usual reluctance of the Jews to accept the gospel. Of all this we hear nothing. There is, however, their encounter with the Jewish sorcerer Elymas, at Paphos, which St Luke has recorded at full length. There is something wrong with the text here, in that the name of Elymas cannot be the translation of Bar-Jesus, as Acts 13:8 suggests, but that need not worry us. What we want to know is the reason St Luke made so much of this event, and nothing of all the other experiences which the apostles must have had on this part of their journey. Two explanations have been offered, the one that the results of the two apostles' efforts had been nil, which is probable, and the other that St Paul changed his name in deference to the Roman proconsul Sergius Paulus, which is also probable, and may even be deduced from Acts 13:9. Neither of these two explanations, however, seems to touch the real matter, although it has to be admitted that the double change of the names of Bar-Jesus to Elymas and of Saul to Paul adds a curious flavour to the affair. We cannot claim to have solved this riddle.

However, judging the report calmly, we must see that the chief event is the blinding of Bar-Jesus. Blinding was the divine punishment for perjurers, who were not punished by human justice, as early as the days of the Hittites. St Paul openly accused Bar-Jesus of this very crime and proved it by blinding him. Bar-Jesus had 'tried to divert the proconsul from the faith' (Acts 13:8). That does not mean that Sergius Paulus had so far contemplated becoming a Christian himself, but that Bar-Jesus had maligned the Christian faith and demanded its suppression. St Paul, being a Roman citizen, brought the proconsul to a decision in favour of the Christians in the island, and thus averted the threat created by Bar-Jesus. The decision was even so favourable that he also received permission to use the proconsul's cognomen of Paul, i.e. he became an honorary member of his household as a 'humble friend' of the Roman noble. One might say, perhaps, that a little snobbery on the part of St Paul was involved here. The direct attack upon Cyprus by St Barnabas and St Paul, we are given to understand by St Luke, had yielded no results; but by indirect means the further development of the Church in the island of Cyprus was assured, at least as long as Sergius Paulus was in office.

It also appears that Sergius Paulus took an intelligent interest in the preaching of St Paul and St Barnabas, for he was 'an intelligent man' (Acts 13:7). This appreciation of him is supported by references to him in the *Natural History* of Pliny the Elder, who quotes him in his second and eighteenth books, where he gives some notes on Cyprus, which may have come from the pen of the proconsul. Pliny's book, having been written in the years between A.D. 65 and 79, may safely be assumed to have referred to our Sergius Paulus. The 'intelligent interest' of the proconsul in the Christian faith did not lead to his baptism; otherwise St Luke would have mentioned it. While Acts 13:12 says nothing about this, however, it suggests that Sergius Paulus did indeed detain St Barnabas and St Paul for a certain length of time, probably in the bad season when shipping was discontinued, in the winter of A.D. 45/6. Thus the stay of the two apostles in the island of Cyprus may well have lasted for the best part of a whole year. This, of course, is conjecture, but yet not a fanciful one, especially if we take into account the boredom which was entailed in the holding of a governorship in the sparsely populated island of Cyprus for a Roman of high birth, who had been used to the excitement of political and court-life at the capital.

IV

The parting from Cyprus took place without any undue ceremony so far as the two apostles were concerned. We remember that they were bound to depart as soon as their task appeared to be accomplished. They travelled to Perga, and there John Mark left them (Acts 13:13). We do not know his reason for doing so, but we are informed in Acts 15:37, 38 that St Paul regarded this as desertion on his part, and we feel that any conjectures as to reasons will be unavailing. It is sufficient to say that the tradition about this quarrel was remembered for a long time by the Church. That is shown by the inclusion of his name in II Tim. 4:11, 'pick up Mark and bring him along with you, for he is of great use in helping me', which is meant to underline and confirm the reconciliation between St Paul and St Mark, presupposed in Col. 4:10 (cf. Phm. 24):

Aristarchus my fellow-prisoner salutes you; so does Mark, the cousin of Barnabas, about whom you have had instructions . . .

Surely, the defection of Mark was a disappointing event; but the two apostles went forward. There followed the great sermon on the Sabbath in the Jewish synagogue at Pisidian Antioch (Acts 13:14 ff.). As usual, we cannot spend our time on analysing St Paul's sermon. It is a difficult one, and also it has not been too well preserved. The interesting thing about it is that, although it takes into account the ignorance on the part of the Jewish leaders at Jerusalem (13:27), it nevertheless contains a strong attack upon them, which yet is not resented by the synagogue at Pisidian Antioch. In short, the direct attack here proves just as unavailing as it did in Cyprus. However, the conflict is joined as soon as the heathen come to listen to St Paul and St Barnabas, thus breaking into the privacy of the Jewish synagogue (Acts 13:45). This reaction was, of course, the logical result of the Jewish privileges within the Empire, which were at once put in jeopardy if the masses attempted to share them. The synagogue was quite willing to admit some 'devout women of high rank' (Acts 13:50), but the mass of the Gentiles had to be kept out. Thus we hear in this context the historical decision of the two apostles made for the first time (Acts 13:46):

The word of God . . . had to be spoken to you in the first instance; but as you push it aside, judging yourselves unworthy of eternal life, well, here we turn to the Gentiles!

Upon this there must have followed a feverish preaching to the Gentiles, and a small church was indeed established among them, as may be seen from the wording of Acts 13:48 f.:

When the Gentiles heard this, they rejoiced and glorified the word of the Lord and believed, that is, all who had been ordained to eternal life; and the word of the Lord went far and wide over the whole country.

We cannot assume that this result could be accomplished in a matter of days, even if the apostles, as is probable, left the missionarizing of the surrounding villages to their enthusiastic disciples. We therefore have to allow about a month for their stay at Pisidian Antioch.

The final effect of the mission to this city was the foundation of a purely Gentile church which was to exist side by side with the Jewish synagogue. Consequently the question of the Jewish privileges did not arise for the new community; but at Iconium this problem had to be faced. Although Acts 14:1 assures us that 'the same thing happened' there, the preaching in the Iconium synagogue seems to have met with a certain amount of response on the part of the Jews: 'a great body both of Jews and Greeks believed', says St Luke. Thus the political problem, which we have outlined, arose there. The apostles had to face the alternative whether the Jews should abandon their privileges, or whether the Gentile Christians should claim them. As a short-term policy the latter was apparently more advisable; but it was doubtful whether it was also sound in view of the years to come. It has always appeared to us as one of the great mysteries of St Paul's mission that he, whose eschatological views filled him with a fervent expectation of Christ's second coming in the very near future, certainly during his own lifetime (I Cor. 15:51: 'here is a secret truth for you: not all of us are to die'), yet favoured the long-time policy of creating a Church for the Gentiles, whereas the presbyters at Jerusalem, who were far less eschatologically minded, hankered after those privileges, which were slowly but surely leading the Synagogue to complete separation from the world in the Jewish ghetto.

Once more we hear of Jewish hostility, which drove the apostles from Iconium (Acts 14:5), and it has been claimed by many scholars that Acts is simply filled with prejudice against the Jews. The French scholar Marcel Simon, a Christian historian at Strasbourg University, has even written a most learned book in which he has set out to prove that the lamb bit the wolf.[1] We have seen that the Jews had good reasons to be afraid of Gentile infiltration, and we must reject this thesis. It still remains to be seen, however, why it was St Paul in particular who was singled out by their wrath. St Luke did not write his book as a glorified life of St Paul, however much he admired him, therefore we have to look for a more objective reason. The answer must surely be that it was he who was the chief preacher of the group of Christian missionaries; and that his Pharisaic training proved him superior to the local rabbis. That appears from the reaction of the people of Lystra at his healing of the lame man. It is perhaps true to say that there is a certain parallelism between the miracles of St Peter and St Paul, as recorded in Acts; but the significance of both their initial miracles is that they herald in the beginning of the Messianic era (Isa. 35:5 f.): 'And then the blind shall see, the deaf shall hear; then shall the lame leap like a deer, and dumb tongues sing for joy' (cf. also Jer. 31:8). Adding to this the name of Hermes, the orator, which the people of Lystra gave to St Paul, it appears clearly that these people saw in him the challenger. So also did the Jews.

Let it be said in fairness that they were called upon to make a most momentous decision, for which they were not equipped. With some justice they felt infuriated by the necessity of deciding for themselves whether or not the fulness of time had come upon them, as St Paul and St Barnabas proclaimed; and they reacted accordingly. It seemed so natural that they should try to eliminate the disturbing factors that out of the blue had descended upon them. It seemed so easy too to deal with them. Their mouths had to be stopped. What concern of the Gentiles was it to hear of 'the living God who made the heaven and the earth and all that in them is' (Acts 14:15)? They ought to be satisfied with their idol-worship. Most of them were so anyhow, as was to be seen by the quick reaction with which they responded to the Jewish call to violence (Acts 14:19).

Thus St Paul was stoned—not, of course, according to the Jewish law; but the plan to do so probably came from the Jews. For stoning disposes of all inquiry for any individual murderer; and this recognition was the cause for the provision of this form of capital punishment by the Jewish law. 'However, as the disciples gathered round him, he got up and went into the town' (Acts 14:20). All the same, St Paul's life was still in danger, and so they all left for Derbe. This escape was a curious one, for whereas Lystra was off the great Roman road through Asia

[1] M. Simon, *Verus Israel* (Paris, 1948).

Minor, Derbe and Iconium, from which the danger came, were right on it. We may state that the boldest plan proved to be the safest as the Jews from Iconium had shot their bolt and did not repeat it. But there may have been another reason too. It seems probable that the year A.D. 46 was now far advanced, and that during the inclement season communications between the two cities were made difficult by wintry conditions. This would also account for the apparent inactivity of the apostles at Derbe, to which Acts 14:22 seems to testify.

If this hypothesis is accepted, it would have been in March, A.D. 47, at the earliest that the apostles made their return journey. With great courage they visited Lystra, Iconium and Pisidian Antioch, and they were not molested. The separation of the churches from the synagogues there had become an accomplished fact by now. Thus the apostles took the opportunity of establishing the church organization, and avoided the synagogues. In the organization of these churches St Barnabas made his influence felt. 'They chose presbyters for them in every church, and with prayer and fasting entrusted them to the Lord in whom they had believed' (Acts 14:23). 'Presbyters', we remember, was the name of the ministers at Jerusalem. At Antioch they had 'prophets and teachers' (Acts 13:1). Therefore we conclude that it was the influence of St Barnabas which made itself felt in the creation of a presbyterate in the churches in the interior of Asia Minor. For St Paul adopted the Antiochene scheme, as we learn from I Cor. 12:28: 'God has set people within the church to be first of all apostles, secondly prophets, thirdly teachers.' Moreover, there is in Acts only one further instance of presbyters in a Gentile church: Acts 20:17, 'he sent to Ephesus for the presbyters of the church', and that is quickly amended to 'bishops' (Moffatt says 'guardians') in 20:28. When St Paul missionarized on his own, therefore, he did not ordain 'presbyters'.

We assume that this organization of the four churches may have taken two months, from March to May of A.D. 47, and that the apostles reached the coast of Asia Minor some time in June. By the middle of July, A.D. 47, therefore, they may have been back in Antioch, to give account of their work to that church from which they had been sent out. We may well wonder how warm their reception actually was. St Luke says nothing about it, and that seems to be an eloquent silence. In fact, a considerable change had come over that church during the years of the apostles' absence. Jerusalem seems to have tightened its grip considerably upon the church at Antioch from where the mission to the Gentiles had first begun.

V

Certain individuals came down from Jerusalem and taught the brothers that 'unless you get circumcised after the custom of Moses, you cannot be saved' (Acts 15:1).

These 'certain individuals' played indeed the most disturbing part in the early Church. St Paul, their most determined opponent, calls them (Gal. 2:4) 'traitors of false brethren, who had crept in to spy out the freedom we enjoy in Christ Jesus; they did aim at enslaving us again'. We have also heard him complain about the same disturbing influences in Phil. 3:18 f.; we also hear of them in II Cor. 11:20 f. St Paul moreover discusses the same problem with the Roman Church in Rom. 2:25 ff. Col. 2:16 ff. also refers to it, and it is only in the two Epistles to the Thessalonians that the matter does not seem to arise. We therefore have to conclude that these 'certain individuals' belonged to a most determined Judaeo-Christian group, which viewed the work of the two apostles, and especially that of St Paul, with serious misgivings. We also hear in Acts 15:5 which group that was:

Some of the believers who belonged to the Pharisaic party got up and said, 'Gentiles must be circumcised and charged to observe the law of Moses.'

We have often wondered whether the sayings of Jesus against the Pharisees may not have been preserved so fully as they are in the canonical Gospels in order to apply an efficient curb upon these very 'believers who belonged to the Pharisaic party'; but we must leave this undiscussed here.

The Antiochene Church decided, as we have seen, to send St Barnabas and St Paul with the relief for the Jerusalem Church; and it appears that they received instructions at the same time to represent its views on the necessity or otherwise of the circumcision of Gentile Christians. St Paul's saying, 'I took Titus with me also' (Gal. 2:1), does no more than implement St Luke's remark that 'Paul and Barnabas along with some others' (Acts 15:2) were sent to Jerusalem. Titus was presumably the only uncircumcised Christian of sufficient standing to join the deputation; and since St Paul claims credit for taking him, it may also be assumed that he had found Titus the only Gentile Christian prepared to force the issue. Such may be derived from St Paul's triumphant remark, 'even my companion Titus, Greek though he was, was not obliged to be circumcised' (Gal. 2:3).

The journey through Phoenicia and Samaria, we feel, could not have been made the triumphant procession that St Luke (Acts 15:3) claims it to have been if the mission from Antioch had not brought the relief to Jerusalem, of which Acts 11:30 speaks, but became so because it showed the loyalty of the Gentile converts to the mother Church at Jerusalem. For in those districts the question of Gentile converts was not an urgent one. St Luke (Acts 11:19) tells us that the mission in Phoenicia had only gone to the synagogues, and Samaria was a special case anyhow. However, the relief from abroad was a necessity for all these churches, and as Jerusalem received support from those Gentiles, the plight of the surrounding districts would also be remembered. We recall St Paul's remark (Gal. 2:10): 'Only, we were to "remember the poor". I was quite eager to do that myself.' In such a setting the reference to the iniquity of demanding that these Gentiles should be circumcised found indeed open ears—to be forgotten as soon as economic circumstances changed for the better.

For the same reason the first meetings between the deputation from Antioch and the Jerusalem Christians did not touch that sore point, but gave St Paul and St Barnabas a chance to report 'how God had been with them and what he had done' (Acts 15:4). It is indeed the contention of the codex 'D' edition of Acts 15, that St Barnabas and St Paul were cited as defendants before the tribunal of 'the apostles and presbyters at Jerusalem' (verse 4); and if that were the case, the meetings mentioned in Acts 15:4 would be difficult to account for; but if, as we maintain, St Barnabas and St Paul brought the relief from Antioch with them, it was only natural to postpone the discussion of the less agreeable part of their mission as long as possible, and to try in the meantime to even out the differences by private discussions. These private discussions did indeed take place, as we learn from Gal. 2:2, 'I submitted the gospel I am in the habit of preaching to the Gentiles, submitting it privately to the authorities', and it appears that the full-dress debate, described by St Luke, only took place to show the complete agreement of the Church leaders.

This might not have come off, for there were those tiresome 'members of the Pharisaic party', who began to voice their opinion. The 'apostles and presbyters' had to retire and to decide how they should be dealt with (Acts 15:6). However, the disturbers were then duly scotched by St Peter and St James of Jerusalem, who acted with remarkable unanimity. It has often been stated that the two speeches, in Acts 15:7 ff. by St Peter, and in Acts 15:13 ff. by St James of Jerusalem, have in fact little to do with that 'keen controversy' reported in Acts 15:7. It is obvious that they gave little attention to what was apparently a very determined resistance on the part of a strong group, if not the majority, amongst the Jerusalem Christians. On the other hand, all this is very true to life. St Peter was stung to the quick that he had to defend once more the individual decision which he had taken in the case of the centurion Cornelius, and St James of Jerusalem was determined to uphold the agreement which he had reached with St Paul. It was he who decided the issue, as St Luke wants us to understand; and those 'members of the Pharisaic party' who, according to St Paul (Gal. 2:12), had claimed his support in A.D. 43 at Antioch, were sadly disappointed. The times had changed, and the Church at Jerusalem could not afford to disown the Gentile churches which had just rescued the Church in Judaea from starvation. Moreover, the eschatological arguments of St Paul seem to have had their effect upon St James, as may be seen from his quotation of Amos 9:11 f. in Acts 15:16 ff. That, at any rate, is what St Luke wants us to understand. Consequently the decision of the Jerusalem Church did after all abide by the suggestion of James, who yet inserted some salve for the wounded consciences of his disappointed stalwarts. All this, if we may say so, is amazingly similar to Church practice ever since.

It is significant that this decision of the Jerusalem Church was couched in language typical of the legislation not only of the Greek city-state, but also of the Roman authorities. Assuming, as we do, that this was actually St Luke's invention, it is nevertheless characteristic of the Church of those early days that it saw itself as a political organization. It is equally important to notice that the decision was made on behalf of 'the brother-hood', as Moffatt translates it. We would perhaps prefer to translate Acts 15:23, 'the apostles and presbyters, your brothers'; but the really important thing is that the decision as it is worded does not indicate that it was taken on behalf of the Jerusalem Church. On the other hand, it did not venture either to maintain that it was the ultimate verdict of the universal Church, and the insertions of St James of Jerusalem never obtained universal acceptance. Thus not even 'D' made such a claim outright, but circumscribed it by inserting the 'golden rule', a doubtful manœuvre. It was essentially a Jerusalem decision.

St Barnabas and St Paul returned to Antioch, and it appears from the Epistle to the Galatians, how St Paul even after several years felt sore at having been worsted at Jerusalem by St James; yet St James with the limited insight he seems to have possessed had expressed clearly, by demanding no more than the observance of the Noachite food-laws, that he too regarded the Church as universal. St Paul's fury, therefore, broke over St Barnabas and John Mark (Acts 15:37 f.). In a quieter mood, he was later to write to the Romans (Rom. 14:20):

You must not break down God's work for the mere sake of food! Everything may be clean, but it is wrong for a man to prove a stumbling-block by what he eats.

For indeed St Paul's view was victorious at Jerusalem, if only after his heroic efforts in founding the Gentile Church.

8   St Paul and the Greeks

In the last lecture we have discussed the legal status of the Church and the Synagogue within the Roman Empire at the parting of their ways during the first missionary journey of St Paul. We have seen how the mark of circumcision was at the same time giving the Jews a privilege, but also restricting them to a life within the boundaries of that privileged area, precluding them from converting the world. The Church was greatly tempted to accept that self-same status. Considerations of conscience as well as of prudence counselled it to follow that way, and it was not only the courage of St Paul, but also the clear insight of St Peter and St James of Jerusalem that the mission to the Gentiles had become a fact, which made for the distinction between the ministry to the circumcision, entrusted to St Peter, and the ministry to the uncircumcised, of which St Paul was put in charge (Gal. 2:7, 8). Whether or not this remark entailed that St Peter, whom we have last seen in charge of the Churches in Judaea (Acts 9:31, 32), was also launched upon a wider field of enterprise, or whether he had already before then contemplated extending his activities to the synagogues of the dispersion, need not worry us here.

We are only concerned in this part of Acts with St Paul who, once more, was staying at Antioch (Acts 15:35), especially as there are various uncertainties about this second stay there. The whole journey back from Jerusalem to Antioch is shrouded in some mystery. We have already concluded that John Mark took part in it. At any rate, we have a wide field of speculation here, since nothing is said about the way in which the decision in Acts 15:22, that the envoys from Jerusalem should accompany the two apostles, was carried out. Perhaps they went by sea, as St Luke does not mention any preaching in Samaria on the way back to Antioch, as he had done for the journey to Jerusalem (Acts 15:3). As we have said before, the churches there were not vitally concerned with the outcome of the apostles' deliberations. They were in any case Christians of the circumcision. We have already seen that it is likely that the preaching of the two apostles on their way to Jerusalem avoided the controversial subject of the circumcision of the Gentiles, but rather dealt with the relief sent to the churches of Jerusalem and Judaea. However that may be, we hear nothing of any publication of the findings of the apostles' council before the arrival of the delegation from Jerusalem at Antioch.

The second great trouble is that St Luke reports of the envoys from Jerusalem (Acts 15:33):

> Then after some time had passed the brothers let them go with a greeting of peace to those who had sent them.

For, on the other hand, we read only a few lines later (Acts 15:39 f.):

> So in irritation they parted company, Barnabas taking Mark with him and sailing for Cyprus, while Paul selected Silas and went off, commended by the brothers to the grace of the Lord.

How, we ask, was he able to do that, if Silas had been despatched, only 'some days earlier', together with Judas Barsabbas, to Jerusalem? This question led as early as the second century to the insertion of the spurious verse, Acts 15:34,[1] which is rightly left out in Moffatt's translation.

Commentators are divided: some assuming that Silas had returned from Jerusalem (de Wette-Overbeck[2]), others making a desperate stand for the genuineness of 15:34, if not in words then in substance, that Silas stayed behind (Zahn[3]). We would rather prefer to be ignorant one way or the other and to point out that this discrepancy is the mark of division between the report of the apostles' council, for which St Luke used earlier material, and that of St Paul's second missionary journey, for the earlier part of which St Luke had no such material. It is for this reason that we assume that no record of St Paul's second visit to the Churches of Pisidia and Lycaonia has been kept. St Luke knew no more than that St Paul this time travelled by land 'through Syria and Cilicia' (Acts 15:41). These words are so reminiscent of Gal. 1:21, 'then I went to the districts of Syria and Cilicia', that it seems to be our duty to find some connection between the two. As a matter of fact these words are the reason why we claim that St Paul did not spend a number of years in inactivity at Tarsus. For there is no record in Acts that any churches had been founded in those regions. Thus, unless we accept the evidence from

---

[1] Cf. AV: 'Notwithstanding it pleased Silas to abide there still.'
[2] W. M. L. de Wette, *Kurze Erklärung der Apostelgeschichte*[4], ed. F. Overbeck (Leipzig, 1870), *ad loc.*
[3] T. Zahn, *Die Apostelgeschichte des Lucas*[4] (Leipzig, 1927), *ad loc.*

Galatians in the way we have suggested, we would have no means of explaining how it happened that there were any 'brothers' at all in Syria and Cilicia for St Paul to strengthen (Acts 15:41).

There is, secondly, the incident of the circumcision of Timothy (Acts 16:3), which demands our attention. St Luke has shown us there how strongly the decision of Jerusalem affected even a man like St Paul. It had been agreed, according to St Paul (Gal. 2:7), that there was to be a different ministry to the uncircumcised from that to the circumcised; and since according to the Jewish Law the status of the mother was decisive, St Paul made up his mind to keep to the letter of the Jerusalem agreement which, 'as they travelled on from town to town, they handed over to the people' (Acts 16:4). This has always and rightly been regarded as the farthest concession which St Paul ever was to make to the Jerusalem Christians. Its bitter fruits can be tasted in his Epistle to the Galatians which, according to Sir William Ramsay, was sent to these very churches in Southern Galatia.[1] St Paul had to refer there (Gal. 2:3) to the example of Titus, because the circumcision of Timothy had indeed opened the door for Judaistic influences. That was not, we believe, because the Galatians coveted the privileges granted to Jews by the Roman authorities for themselves—that was rather the point of the Judaizers from Jerusalem—but because they were eager to have no less grace than St Paul's great favourite Timothy.

II

However, these churches in the interior of Asia Minor were yet only a backwater. One hundred years later, indeed, their importance for the whole Catholic Church was made clear by an outbreak of prophetic inspiration in these churches in the middle of the second century A.D. It threatened to split the whole Catholic Church from East to West. But as yet this development lay in the far future. It might have been the plan of St Paul to found a great Church throughout Asia Minor, and some scholars have taken Acts 16:6 f., mentioning the provinces where St Paul was stopped by the Holy Spirit from preaching the gospel, as an indication pointing that way. They are Phrygia, Galatia, Mysia, Bithynia and Asia, the proconsular province of Asia, a list similar to that in I Pet. 1:1, 'Pontus, Galatia, Cappadocia, Asia and Bithynia.' We feel that

[1] W. M. Ramsay, *Historical Commentary on St Paul's Epistle to the Galatians* (London, 1899).

this exegesis is a little fanciful. Anyhow, St Paul's goal was in Europe (Acts 16:9):

A vision appeared to Paul by night, the vision of a Macedonian standing and appealing to him with the words, 'Cross over to Macedonia to help us.'

This, we can say with some assurance, happened in A.D. 51, and some years ago Greece celebrated the 1900th anniversary of the event by the issue of a special set of stamps; but it would be ludicrous to deny that Christianity had spread to the European continent before. It had even been preached to the Gentiles there, at Rome for instance; the significance of St Paul's coming to Europe lay only in the fact that he, as the apostle of the Gentiles, was sent by the Holy Spirit to confirm this development.

Thus St Paul came on the usual trade-way from Troas to Neapolis-Kavalla, and went to Philippi. It seems somewhat surprising that, in spite of his vision, his method of approach had not changed in the least. Moffatt's translation rests on unsafe ground in two respects: 'The river' in Acts 16:13 should be questioned, because there are only some little streams near Philippi, and also 'where as usual there was a place of prayer'. 'Where we believed a place of prayer would be', is a better reading. Both these points are important, because in Acts 16:10 St Luke begins his 'we-report', i.e. claims to be an eye-witness. St Paul and his companions had no more success than the conversion of one woman, 'Lydia, a dealer in purple, who belonged to the town of Thyatira' (Acts 16:14 f.).

However, by God's mercy, the daemons began to profess their fear of Christ. Men, so we are given to understand by St Luke, were on the whole too dull to see that the preacher of salvation had come; but the evil spirit which possessed a poor lunatic slave-girl made her cry out, 'These men are servants of the Most High God, they proclaim to you the way of salvation!' (Acts 16:17). Our scientific age will explain this by reference to the excitability of mentally diseased people, which is on the whole no more than a translation of ancient into modern terms. It does not explain to us in what way that slave-girl was abnormal, nor answer the question what we should understand by 'normality'. Neither does it help, but rather hinders, our understanding of the incident here described. Insanity is a religious problem, even if doctors will not recognize it as such. It is 'abnormal' because it prevents the patient from seeing the world for what it is, namely as the living creation of God. If modern science will continue to neglect attempts at appreciating the meaning of this world and of our life in it, it may well lose the ability of distinguishing between mental health and mental disease. Even now our clever psychologists, outlining the various types of human dispositions as religious, scientific and God knows what, are successfully obscuring the limits between mental health and mental disease. For they deny that there may be anything objective in truth or love, liberty or responsibility, and thus admit of no other basis for judging mental health than their own enormous wisdom.

To turn back to St Paul: he in his annoyance ejected the daemon without anybody asking him to do so—what became of the poor girl we are left to guess—and that set things moving. There followed the arrest of St Paul and Silas, their being accused of damage to other people's property, their summary punishment by flogging, and their imprisonment (Acts 16:18–24). We are so conversant with the story that its significance seems to escape us completely. Let us consider it more closely: the apostle of Jesus Christ performed in his Master's name a great miracle of healing (Acts 16:18). Instead of giving thanks to God for his mercy, the people who have charge of the poor sick person murmur and regard it as an unwarranted interference; and the mob agrees with them. The apostle and his friend are beaten up and gaoled at the order of a crooked court; and all that appears to everybody concerned, magistrates and mob, gaoler and apostle, as a perfectly normal thing, which might have happened anywhere—and does so happen to this day all over the world.

Only God did not seem to be pleased with such a state of affairs, where his gift of healing is used in annoyance, where his merciful salvation is regarded as damage to property, where justice is perverted and his apostle tortured; and therefore he sends an earthquake (Acts 16:25 f). Modern scientific stupidity will rapidly assert that the district of Philippi has long been subject to frequent earthquakes, as indeed it is, and that therefore the causal connection between these acts of human perversity and a natural phenomenon like an earthquake has nothing to commend it. St Luke was a scientist too, we assume, and he knew these arguments, since they were already well-known at his time. He might even have added that, if every such perversion of morals and justice were to cause an earthquake, then indeed the whole earth would be constantly shaking everywhere; but in this case he found the causal connection proved by the conversion of the gaoler of Philippi. For, he would argue, it is quite as absurd to assume that there should never be a moral meaning to an earthquake, as it would be to attach such a meaning to it always. Thus St Luke wants us to understand that this earthquake was the sign of

God's forgiving wrath, by which the first Greek, the gaoler of Philippi, was won for the gospel of Christ (Acts 16:32 ff.).

This recognition makes us all the more aware of the moral problem involved in St Paul's subsequent behaviour. Was he right to exact such strict justice from the magistrates of Philippi? Opinions are very much divided, more so in this country than elsewhere. Perhaps it may be permitted to state our own feelings in this matter, especially since St Luke gives no indication as to the rights or wrongs of the case. To us, unrepentant sinners, it gives indeed great satisfaction that these magistrates were duly chastened. They were the exponents of that order which St Luke characterized so scathingly in Acts 16:19–24, and yet they did not even know how to play their own instrument. They never expected that the class-distinctions which they were eager to uphold could be turned against them. The whole second half of Acts 16 must be understood as a bitter satire on social conditions within the Roman Empire. The magistrates of Philippi, quite an important place in its time, are made to bow first to the disreputable owners of the slave-girl, and on the very next day to their victims, in both cases because they were afraid for their position. Such was the type of civil servants of the earthly Emperor. We feel strongly that St Paul was right to give his new converts an idea of the time-serving that was going on amongst these officials, especially to the gaoler who, for fear of these little despots, had almost committed suicide.

III

It was St Paul's favourite Church which he had founded at Philippi, but as soon as it was established he had to leave it. He went along the Roman road, the *Via Egnatia*, to the great harbour and commercial centre of Thessalonica. There his activities were once more confined to the Jewish synagogue with its numerous proselytes, which, of course, was asking for trouble, especially since the mob was once more quickly roused against the Christians by the Jews. These events were by and large a repetition of the happenings at Pisidian Antioch and Iconium. They therefore need not occupy us very long. There was, however, one new feature here. As in Philippi, so at Thessalonica the Christians were brought before the magistrates. We have to take notice of this difference. In Asia Minor the varnish of civilization and the *pax Romana* was still very thin. Violence to strangers came naturally to those people who for centuries had been forced to protect themselves from the raids of the savages in the hills, as well as from the warring kings and feudal lords. Greece, however, was pacified. The mob had been accustomed to go to court or else to the police. At Philippi, a Roman colony (Acts 16:12), they even knew how to make a charge. At Thessalonica, however, no legal charge was brought forward. What the mob shouted was, according to Acts 17:6 f.:

These upsetters of the whole world have come here too! Jason has welcomed them! They all violate the decrees of Caesar by declaring someone else called Jesus is king.

Here we stop. For indeed this accusation is astounding. This mob at Thessalonica apparently knew something about the gospel; and they had not learned it from St Paul, or at any rate not only from St Paul. They knew about it from 'the decrees of Caesar', and that means from decrees of the Emperor Claudius. What decrees were they? The most likely answer is that they were the very ones by which the Jews had been banished from Rome because of their rioting *impulsore Chresto*, as we have learned from Suetonius.[1] They were probably also the decrees by which Aquila and Priscilla had been dislodged from Rome (Acts 18:2). The mob thus regarded the differences between St Paul and the synagogal Jews at Thessalonica as an internal quarrel of the Jews, and was determined to side with that party which was loyal to the Emperor. Moreover, it must have assumed that the newcomers had arrived from the West, and that was probably the reason why they did not recognize St Paul. Still more surprising, however, is this: St Paul neither at Philippi nor at Thessalonica did what he had done before at Pisidian Antioch and Derbe, and preached to the Gentiles. We can only guess the reason for this: the influence of the Jerusalem decision in the person of the Jerusalemite Silas—or is it to be assumed that no Gentile in these regions of Macedonia ever asked him for instruction?

IV

In any case, St Paul had to leave Thessalonica for Beroea, and there followed a time of rest and of moderate success (Acts 17:10 ff.), still on the same lines. Beroea is a small town in the hills, a good way from Thessalonica, not much more than a big village. However, it had a

[1] See p. 65.

synagogue, and its members were willing to listen to St Paul. Nevertheless, the hue and cry was on. The Jews from Thessalonica heard of St Paul's work at Beroea. Did they have some right of supervising the synagogues in the neighbourhood? We have no means of answering this question, because we know hardly anything about the organization of the Jews of the dispersion. All that St Luke has to tell us is that 'they came to create a disturbance and a riot among the crowds at Beroea also' (Acts 17:13); and that looks very much like a biased statement. However that may be, St Paul had to leave Beroea. It is difficult to account for Moffatt's translation in Acts 17:14, 'on his way to the sea'. St Paul could hardly have gone by sea, as the harbour for Beroea is Thessalonica; and the road to Athens from the north passes through Beroea. Something is amiss here, as is shown by I Thess. 3:1, 2:

I made up my mind to be left behind at Athens all alone; I sent Timotheus[1] our brother, a minister of God in the gospel of Christ, for your strengthening and encouragement in the faith . . .

This evidently disagrees with Acts 17:14, 'Silas and Timotheus remained where they were', and we can do no more than lay our finger on the spot where the disagreement occurs. It appears that Timothy's instructions (Acts 17:15) included a visit to Thessalonica. There is nothing to indicate that Timothy was sent from Athens to Thessalonica in I Thess. 3:2.

Thus St Paul was separated from his Jewish companions, Silas and Timothy, at Athens; and there he 'argued in the synagogue with the Jews . . . and also in the market place daily with those who chanced to be present' (Acts 17:17). It may be no more than a suspicion that St Paul felt less hampered without their company; but however that may have been, his new policy met with the most crushing failure. Whether or not his famous sermon was meant as a defence against an accusation that he was 'a herald of foreign gods' (Acts 17:18), delivered before the supreme court at Athens on the Areopagus, as Cadbury thinks,[2] is at least a moot question. We are not convinced that the words quoted were even consciously fashioned after the accusation brought against Socrates: 'perverting the youths and not believing in the gods of the city, but in other new deities'. At any rate their cases were different, since St Paul was not an Athenian, but a foreigner not bound by law to worship the city

---

[1] Moffatt retains the classical form 'Timotheus' in his translation, instead of the anglicized 'Timothy'.

[2] H. J. Cadbury, *The Book of Acts in History* (New York, 1955), pp. 44 f., 51 ff.

gods. We would rather assume that 'the Areopagus' denotes the hill where the court customarily met, rather than the court itself, and that St Paul's sermon was introduced as a philosophical discourse given in a public place. There was no trial by court.

Once more we have to state that the sermon in Acts 17:22–31 is not of St Luke's making, but a traditional outlining of the missionary approach to Greeks. Once more we refrain from analysing it, and only state that St Luke wants us to understand that it failed completely. The number of converts at Athens was small, because the Athenians remained convinced that the wisdom of the world, their philosophy, was preferable to the foolishness of God (I Cor. 1:18 f.) and rejected St Paul's assertion that 'God ranks this world's wisdom as sheer folly' (I Cor. 3:19). These remarks as well as that in Col. 2:8, 'beware of anyone getting hold of you by philosophy and vain deceit'[1] (Moffatt's is a commentary rather than a translation!), written from Rome at a much later time, still show how St Paul smarted under that defeat.

However, Athens was not Greece, just as little as Oxford is England. Once more (and that is indeed something which St Luke will never cover up, however great his admiration for St Paul), the apostle had misjudged the situation. It is being misjudged to this day. Athens, the philosophy of the great Greek men of thought, is still erroneously identified with the Greeks, and the achievement of those universal minds is contrasted as 'Greek', and therefore invalid, with the 'Hebrew', and therefore valid, thought of the talmudic Rabbis. This is one of the most serious heresies of modern theology. St Paul did not go to the Jewish synagogues because in their thought they were so close to Jesus, but because the gospel had to be preached first to the Jews, and after that to the Greeks (Rom. 1:16).

The deep depression of St Paul after his failure at Athens may be seen from I Thessalonians. He left the city quietly, without founding a Church, to go to Corinth (Acts 18:1); and there Eastern and Western Christianity met in the persons of St Paul and Aquila and Priscilla, the latter much subdued by their banishment from Rome (18:2). It was the year A.D. 52/3, and the decree of Claudius had been proclaimed in A.D. 49/50, if we may trust the later Christian historian Orosius (vii. 6:15). There is no mention made in Acts of a conversion of those two by St Paul, and as we learn from Rom. 16:3 and I Cor. 16:19 that they were Christians, the conclusion is that they were such already when St Paul met them. St Luke did not say anything about that for two reasons:

[1] Moffatt: '. . . by means of a theosophy which is specious make-believe'.

first, because the Church at Corinth was St Paul's foundation (I Cor 3:6, 'I did the planting'), and secondly, because he did not wish to enter into any explanations as to the reasons why Aquila and Priscilla had not preached the gospel since they had settled at Corinth. The description of Aquila as 'a Jew' (Acts 18:2) cannot be adduced as a statement about his religion.

At Corinth we hear for the second time the Pauline verdict on the Jews (Acts 18:6):

Your blood be on your own heads! I am not responsible! After this I will go to the Gentiles.

It is important in these words to hear judgment pronounced on the Jews, just as in Acts 13:46 it was pronounced on the Jews at Pisidian Antioch, by the power given by Jesus Christ to his apostles. We have to keep in mind his saying in Luke 10:12, 'I tell you, on the great Day it will be more bearable for Sodom than for that town.' Having said some hard things about the Judaizers in our last lecture, we should add here, that at least one of their intentions was to make the Christian faith more accessible to their fellow-Jews by imposing at least part of the Law upon the Gentiles. We have to remember also the solemn warning spoken by God through His prophet (Ezek. 3:18), 'If you say nothing to warn the wicked ... that wicked man shall die for his iniquity, but I will hold you responsible for his death,' which is openly alluded to in these two passages of Acts. It was the apostles' power of binding which St Paul used in both cases. It was a most serious matter for both parties that the apostle should now at the last turn to the Greeks.

Who were these Greeks? It is interesting to notice that St Luke makes no attempt here to contrast the people of Athens with those of Corinth. We only gather from St Paul's vision in Acts 18:9, 10 ('I have many people in this city') and the conscious imitation of Josh. 1:9 ('be firm and brave ... for the Eternal, your God is with you') in the words 'for I am with you', that here lay the turning point, prophesied by Hosea 2:23; 'to No-folk I will say "My-folk", and they shall say, "Thou art my God".' It is only when we turn to St Paul's Epistles to the Corinthians that we can appreciate what manner of men they were. St Luke provides us with the framework by which the facts presupposed in these Epistles may be filled in; and his description of the Greeks is left over till we come to St Paul's stay at Ephesus. The eighteen months during which St Paul lived with Aquila and Priscilla at Corinth (Acts 18:11) are punctuated only by the one event of Gallio's refusal to adjudicate between the president of the synagogue, Sosthenes, and St Paul (Acts 18:12–17).

There was no case to answer; nevertheless, St Paul, Priscilla and Aquila left Corinth in A.D. 54. The decrees of Claudius were still in force; the threat of loyalist riots was still hanging over all of them, and St Paul had not forgotten the danger in which he had been at Thessalonica, and so he left Corinth. Various reasons may be given for his decision to do so. One would be fear of what might happen to him; but we would regard that as a secondary consideration. All the same, it was discussed in early Christian circles, as the Gospel shows in the case of Jesus, who 'withdrew' for similar reasons to the regions of Tyre (Matt. 15:21), where He cured the daughter of the Syro-Phoenician woman. The chief point of all these stories about the riots of the Gentiles in Acts, is however to be found in Ps. 2:1, 'why do the nations rage . . .?' St Luke wants to show how the Gentile Church was, so to speak, snatched from the combined hostile power of Jews and heathen. Satan always lay in wait for the apostle, but he attacked him each time just as it was too late, i.e. when he had already succeeded in founding a new Church for Christ. This was one of the fundamental convictions of St Luke, and it does him great credit that at the foundation of the Church at Derbe he did not invent such a clash when it did not happen. However, where a clash did occur, he may have put it at the end of St Paul's ministry, even if it did not quite belong there, as Acts 18:18, 'after staying on for a number of days', shows in the case of Corinth.

There follows the journey to Ephesus, Acts 18:18 ff., for which we are given no elaborate reason. St Paul apparently went there for the sake of his friends Aquila and Priscilla. St Luke has inserted two riddles in this short passage. The first is the vow of Aquila (rather than St Paul, Acts 18:18). We feel that it is meant to illustrate the enormous difficulties encountered by St Paul in founding any Gentile Church. Aquila had listened for almost two years to St Paul's instruction, and nevertheless he carried on with his vow, which after all the Pharisees judged as either totally (Hillel) or at least partly (Shammai) void. Such were St Paul's most loyal followers: filled with only half-digested Jewish lore, shaken by the enmity of the world around them, crying out for some law, the observance of which might assure them of God's grace and mercy towards them. What was to be expected of them for the conversion of the world? The synagogue held them with tentacles which they could not shake off. Even St Paul went again to the synagogue at Ephesus. From there he sailed to Caesarea—an obvious impossibility, for the harbour of

Ephesus was silted up. But St Luke did not join St Paul on this journey. Just as St Paul and St Barnabas could not have landed at Perga (Acts 13:13) because it lay inland, St Paul could not sail from Ephesus. From verses 19 to 23 St Luke enumerates events known only from hearsay.

V

Thus all the numerous conjectures about this journey of St Paul's to Jerusalem, which were begun already in the second century, when Acts 18:21 was given the form it has in the A.V., 'I must by all means keep this feast that cometh in Jerusalem,' are unavailing. So also is any attempt to align this journey to Galatians. It may even be asked whether St Paul went any further than Caesarea—to St Philip. The words 'to the capital' (Acts 18:22), at any rate, are Moffatt's conjecture and not in the Greek. The whole passage is only a conjecture on the part of St Luke himself.

However, St Luke was fully informed about later events at Ephesus. He tells us about Apollos, the Alexandrian Christian, 'who had been instructed in the way of the Lord and preached and taught about Jesus with ardour and accuracy' (Acts 18:25). It is important to take notice of the fact that here the third branch of the Church, Alexandria, was brought into contact with the Roman (Aquila) and the Jerusalem branches. It is also significant that Alexandria is represented as heterodox. 'All the baptism he knew was that of John.' Aquila and Priscilla had to explain 'more accurately to him what the Way of God really meant' (Acts 18:26). There is, however, no mention made that Apollos was re-baptized or at least confirmed like the Samaritans. Let us just state two things in appreciation of the Apollos episode: first, that St Luke did not know I Corinthians, so that he did not mention Apollos's journey because he also appears there (I Cor. 3:5–4:6; 16:12; cf. Tit. 3:13); and secondly, that St Luke saw the chief difference between Alexandrian and Catholic Christianity in their doctrine of baptism.

St Paul was at that time not available to baptize Apollos, for he arrived at Ephesus only after Apollos had gone to Corinth (Acts 19:1). So St Luke, in order to show St Paul's orthodoxy as well as his apostleship, made him baptize and confirm at Ephesus a full dozen of 'disciples', who had neither heard of the Holy Spirit nor of Christian baptism, but only of St John's (Acts 19:1–7). This story is most important. It is generally assumed that these men belonged to a sect founded by St John the Baptist. However, Eduard Meyer[1] has rightly stressed the fact that Acts 18:24–19:7 is the only witness for the existence of a sect of St John the Baptist's disciples. Can we say that it does constitute such evidence? 'Disciple' was a common description of Christians, and there seems to be no reason to doubt that Apollos and those other disciples regarded themselves as Christians, but had nevertheless neither heard of Pentecost nor of Christian baptism as practised by the Jerusalem Church, administered 'in the name of Jesus'. We must remember that even Catholic tradition has refrained from making the Church at Alexandria an apostolic foundation. It has named St Mark as its patron saint. That is another pointer to the fact that Alexandria had rejected the Jerusalem influence, which the Church at Antioch had accepted. It is, therefore, to be assumed that those twelve of Acts 19:7 were Alexandrian Christians, and would have been surprised at being described as 'John's disciples'.

There followed the separation of the Church from the Synagogue at Ephesus during St Paul's two year stay at that city (Acts 19: 8–10). This notice has the intention of determining the whole length of St Paul's sojourn, so that all the events told subsequently should be arranged within that period. Thus Acts 19:21, 22 and 20:1, 2 are only meant as a frame for the story of the riot at Ephesus (Acts 19:23–41). It is to be assumed that the riot at Ephesus did indeed happen at the very moment when St Paul had already made his preparations to leave the city.

However, St Paul's campaign against magic practices within that Church was his chief task, we are given to understand, during his ministry there. About Acts 19:11–19 the commentators of the last century have—as often—asked the correct questions and given the wrong answers. It is correct to state that the miracles of St Paul in Acts 19:12 are recorded in a conscious analogy to those of St Peter in Acts 5:15 f., and serve to enhance his apostleship. However, this recognition is insufficient for the exegesis of our passage. What St Luke really intended was to give a warning against false miracles in the name of Jesus. The passage also is meant to represent to us the first main characteristic of the Greeks at that time. They were insatiable miracle-addicts. The whole passage translates into the setting of the Gentile mission that warning of Jesus (Matt. 7:22 f.):

Many will say to me at that Day, 'Lord, Lord, did we not prophesy in your name? did we not cast out daemons in your name? did we not perform many

---

[1] *Ursprung und Anfänge des Christentums*, iii (Berlin, 1923), pp. 112 f.

miracles in your name?' Then I will declare to them, 'I never knew you; depart from my presence, you workers of iniquity'.

The lesson here, therefore, is not to encourage a cult of St Paul's relics, but to insist that Christianity was not meant as a magic art (Acts 19:18 f.). Needless to say, the magic papyri prove that the name of Jesus was nevertheless frequently invoked by sorcerers.

The second characteristic feature of Greek life in the time of St Paul, we are given to understand, is the incessant rioting of the mob. That is the meaning of the well-known story of the insurrection at Ephesus (Acts 19:23–41). For the historian it contains invaluable information; for theological exegesis, however, only two things need detain us: the point of St Paul's friendship with the Asiarchs (Acts 19:31) and the great length at which the event is reported. Let it suffice to say with regard to the first that it shows that as a Christian St Paul spurned the Pharisaic ideas of ritual purity, which would have excluded such a friendship; and that the Asiarchs' office was a religious one, because of the religious character of the Roman Empire. As regards the second, we can only say that we have drawn the parallel between the attitude of the Jewish mob at Jerusalem at the martyrdom of St Stephen (Acts 6:8 ff.) and the circumstances of the riot at Ephesus already in an earlier lecture[1] and need not add to it.

Thus St Paul for the last time left a Church of his with the daemons of the heathen raging at their defeat. He started on the journey to his own martyrdom, and although this journey still entailed much missionary work among the Greeks, we must leave him there—mainly for lack of time.

---

[1] See p. 49.

9   St Paul and the Jews

I

We left St Paul—too early—in our last lecture on his departure from Ephesus. We can only follow his course in A.D. 56 through Greece as rapidly as St Luke describes it (Acts 20:1–4), although this whole chapter presents us with the main problem of synchronizing St Paul's Epistles with St Luke's narrative. Early in April A.D. 57 'we sailed from Philippi' (Acts 20:6), once more an inexactitude, 'after the days of unleavened bread' (the Passover). There followed the sojourn in Troas with the reference to the celebration of Holy Communion by St Paul (Acts 20:7): 'we met for the breaking of bread', an evening Communion with a prolonged address by St Paul and the miracle of the reviving of Eutychus. This passage is once more fraught with difficulties, which we have to pass over. The one great question is, of course, the miracle itself, reminiscent of the reviving of Tabitha by St Peter (Acts 9:36 ff.), and yet not similar enough to make the thesis fool-proof that it was only recorded to enhance the equal status of St Paul and St Peter. The other is the very celebration of the Eucharist, the breaking of the bread at the end of the service, after midnight (Acts 20:11), the importance of the address, and the general similarity to Jesus's Last Supper, with St Paul also leaving to meet his supreme crisis. However, we must pass over all this.

Next follows the report on St Paul's journey from Troas to Miletus (Acts 20:13–16). We have already stated in an earlier lecture, how St Paul was made 'the traveller' by the command of the Holy Spirit (Acts 13:2, 3), and that these reports on his journeys have a theological meaning. We shall return to this presently; but we have to point out that the whole journey from Philippi to Jerusalem took no more than six weeks, since St Paul was arrested there in the course of Pentecost. Theologically our passage is meant to provide a frame for St Paul's farewell address to the ministers of the Church at Ephesus (Acts 20:17–35), ending with the famous uncanonical saying of Jesus, 'To give is happier than to get' (20:35). This too we have to pass over, although it is an address that St Luke claims to have heard himself, and therefore provides us with an unique opportunity for the assessment of the relations between his own theology and that of St Paul. Once more the spirit of this most moving amongst all the addresses in Acts is that of a final farewell: 'he told them that they would never see his face again' (Acts 20:38).

On goes the journey, and there is something of very great literary art in the inexorable progress marked by the short descriptions of long and weary days aboard ship, which are interspersed between the revelations of spiritual power granted to Christ's apostle, one of which is found once more in Acts 21:1–3. They round off the picture of churches welcoming and sadly dismissing the Apostle. In Acts 21:4 it is the Church at Tyre, one of the places St Paul probably visited on his journey to the apostles' council, when St Barnabas and he travelled through Phoenicia preaching the gospel (Acts 15:3). Here also the first warning is given to St Paul (Acts 21:4):

These disciples told Paul by the Spirit not to set foot in Jerusalem.

Another short description of the remainder of the journey follows (Acts 21:6–8), and at last we find St Paul re-united with his friends at St Philip's house in Caesarea (Acts 21:8).

We know only of one other equally harassing description of a journey in the Bible, the last journey of the prophet Elijah (II Kings 2:1–12). It is impossible to say whether this analogy is intentional or not; but we believe that the warnings of the inspired disciples must be interpreted in this light, and especially that of the prophet Agabus which has such a penetrating Old Testament ring (Acts 21:11):

He came to us, took Paul's girdle and bound his own feet and hands, saying, 'Here is the word of the holy Spirit: So shall the Jews bind the owner of this girdle at Jerusalem and hand him over to the Gentiles'.

What was the force which made St Paul persist in his determination to go up to Jerusalem? More than one student of Acts has claimed that he acted in sheer disobedience to the command of the Holy Spirit. In order to resolve this difficulty we have to make up our mind first about the meaning of these warnings 'in the Spirit', and secondly about St Paul's reasons for disregarding them. Those who reprove St Paul's disobedience to the Spirit disregard the fact that he himself had 'resolved in the Spirit to travel . . . to Jerusalem for the sake of Jesus Christ' (Acts 19:21) and had proclaimed this publicly in his farewell sermon at Ephesus (Acts 20:22 f.):

Now here I go to Jerusalem under the binding force of the Spirit. What is to befall me there, I do not know. Only I know this, in town after town the holy Spirit testifies to me that bonds and troubles are awaiting me.

Thus St Paul regarded the warnings of the Holy Spirit as informative, not as prohibitive warnings. The second question is more difficult to answer because St Luke has left so much unsaid. We can learn nothing from Acts about the way in which St James and the Jerusalem Church had interpreted the decisions of the apostles' council. We can only infer from the words 'for the sake of the Lord Jesus' (Acts 21:13) that St Paul felt that the Church among the Gentiles was in need of much more sympathy from the mother Church. From I Cor. 1:12 and 3:22 we gather that St Peter had preached in the churches of St Paul's foundation, and had perhaps been less tactful than he ought to have been. From various passages in II Corinthians, Philippians and Colossians, we have gathered that Jerusalem interference abroad was on the increase.

However, we have to guard against confusing the two separate issues involved. Modern research has an unwholesome tendency to see in one the two different sets of differences that existed between the Christology of St Paul and of the Jerusalem Church, on the one hand, and their respective doctrines of the validity of the Law of Moses, on the other. The two are, of course, connected, and it is true to say that Jas. 2:17, 'so faith, unless it has deeds, is dead in itself', with its nasty tilt at Gal. 2:16, 'we know that a man is justified simply by faith in Jesus Christ, and not by doing what the Law commands', may have aimed at both. Nevertheless, the varying emphasis put on either the death or the resurrection of Jesus Christ by the two parties is nowhere mentioned as a point of dispute between St Paul and the Jerusalem Church.

II

In a book from which we differ very much in the general appreciation of Acts, Professor S. G. F. Brandon has given a picturesque description of the conflict betweeen St Paul and Jerusalem.[1] In it he insists very rightly upon Acts 21:20–25, their differences about the circumcision; but he also suggests—without any such support from the sources—that it arose from the different Christologies of St Paul[2] and the Jerusalem Church,[3] and thus gives a prime example of the attitude here criticized. For it seems to us a perfectly true statement that the Pauline Christology has not been accepted by the vast majority of Christian theologians as well as laymen to this very day. In fact, my teacher, the late Karl Ludwig

[1] S. G. F. Brandon, *The Fall of Jerusalem and the Christian Church* (London, 1951), pp. 134 ff.   [2] *Op. cit.*, pp. 54 ff.   [3] *Op. cit.*, pp. 74 ff.

Schmidt of Basle, used to say that the Christology of St Paul would be the eternal problem of the Church to the end of time. On the other hand, there is not a shred of evidence that circumcision of the Gentiles was ever demanded by the Church after the Jerusalem council. The main issue had been decided for good, and only the borderline cases remained. Thus St Paul had undoubtedly gained the victory in this matter, and it seems to us a most serious misrepresentation when it is claimed that in actual fact St Paul's work ended in failure at his last visit to Jerusalem.

These preliminary remarks have been necessary, because it has been suggested by the whole school of students believing in a Pauline catastrophe that St Paul had been summoned to Jerusalem in order to justify his actions before the Christian Sanhedrin of presbyters there. This is a very old theory, hinted at already by the 'D' edition of Acts, and especially because of this *retouché* has not very much to commend it. It seems to us more probable that St Paul went to complain about the disloyalty of those 'certain individuals' (Acts 15:1) who still claimed to represent the views of the Jerusalem Church when they urged the Gentiles to accept circumcision. However, the key to the whole situation, we feel, is provided for us by the words of Acts 19:21: 'after these events Paul resolved in the Spirit to travel . . . to Jerusalem.' What events were they? The one was the admission of the Alexandrian Christians to the Catholic Church (Acts 19:1–7). We remember that Alexandria had rejected control by the Jerusalem apostles so that there lay a point of friction. The second was the stand St Paul had taken against the 'Jewish high priest' Sceva and his sons (Acts 19:14 ff.). Hypothetically we would connect this with Luke 11:19, 'by whom do your sons cast them out?' and 11:23, 'he who is not with me is against me'. However that may be, Sceva, if he was a priest, must have come from Jerusalem, and was probably in the opinion of the Jerusalem Church a sympathizer, if not a Christian. The case of Luke 9:49 f., with Jesus's saying, 'he who is not against you is for you', is also very similar. Both these steps demanded an amicable settlement with the Jerusalem Church.

Thus St Paul took the bull by the horns when he arrived at Jerusalem, and the reply of the presbyters (Acts 21:20–25) is obviously apologetic. They maintain, with what good faith we do not know, their loyalty to the Jerusalem agreement (Acts 15:28 f.), but they plead their difficulties in upholding it amongst their followers, especially if St Paul, as a Jew, a Christian of the circumcision himself, had discarded his respect for the Law. They stress 'how many thousands of believers there are among the Jews, all of them ardent upholders of the Law' (Acts 21:20), because they feel that they are already outnumbered not only by the Gentile Christians, but also by the 'Jews who live among the Gentiles' and would be willing 'to break away from Moses and not to circumcise their children' (Acts 21:21), one of the borderline cases. It seems uncritical to neglect the fact that the activities of St Paul must have worried the Church at Jerusalem considerably more than their little pin-pricks annoyed the temperamental apostle. The two other points were not yet brought up, but they make us understand why St Paul was agreeable to an incontrovertible proof of his loyalty to the Jerusalem agreement.

III

Unless we seriously take into account the dangerous situation in which the Jerusalem Church found itself because of the constant complaints about St Paul's activities pouring in from abroad at the Jewish Sanhedrin and the high priest's offices, we shall not understand the desperate counsel which they gave to St Paul. For the suggestion made by certain scholars that they intended to trap St Paul has no evidence to support it, and is refuted by internal evidence. Alexandria had rejected the Jerusalem influence; whether Rome had established its full relationship with the mother Church is at least uncertain; what those Cypriotes and Cyrenians, who had started from Antioch to missionarize the Gentiles, were doing at the time is unknown, but that their activities had completely ceased seems improbable. Only one thing is certain, that it was St Paul who alone of all the missioners to the Gentiles had entered into an agreement with Jerusalem. He was by no means just a liability to the Jerusalem Church; in the field of the mission to the Gentiles he was its one great asset.

Thus we feel that it is not unreasonable to assume that the Jerusalem presbyters honestly believed that a show of legal piety on the part of St Paul would clear up what animosity there existed against him amongst the Jerusalem Christians. Neither is it so unreasonable to believe that he who wrote (I Cor. 9:20),

To Jews I have become like a Jew, to win over Jews; to those under the Law I have become as one of themselves—though I am not under the Law myself— to win over those under the Law,

should have consented to follow out their suggestion. However, St Paul in so doing exposed himself to a danger from quarters over which the

Jerusalem Church had no control. The presbyters were probably sufficiently well informed about the feelings of the Jerusalem Jews, but since the time of St Stephen the Jews from abroad were an unknown factor. The analogy between St Stephen's martyrdom and the disaster which befell St Paul is undeniable, but St Luke's report of it is quite independent. Jews from Asia who had come to the Feast of Weeks, Pentecost, recognized St Paul amongst the crowd in the temple (Acts 21:27) and detained him. Evidently the Jerusalem Christians felt unable to protect him and—vanished.

Up to 21:27–29 the language of the 'we-report' is clearly discernible. From 21:30 onwards, however, St Luke relied upon a written source, which is different in style. We can only guess who may have been responsible for its compilation. It seems improbable that it came from the Church at Jerusalem, for it contains no explanation of its complete inactivity after the disaster. Some excuse at least for the disappearance of all the thousands of Jerusalem Christians was surely called for. The silence of Acts about them is an eloquent mark of disapproval. St Luke, therefore, drew probably on notes of another member of the Pauline circle, mentioned in Acts 20:4, who was present in the temple at the time of the catastrophe. St Luke himself, we take it, was prevented from going there because he was a Gentile Christian. Now the only one who was qualified to be there among those mentioned in Acts 20:4 was Timothy, and thus we conclude that Acts 21:30–40 may have come from his pen. This is, of course, by no means certain, but it seems a sounder principle to try to find a possible author than to resort to an anonymous one. His report is precise and to the point: the Hellenists got hold of St Paul, charging him with an offence against the Roman regulation which declared the Jerusalem temple enclosure to be out of bounds for Gentiles (Acts 21:27 ff.). The 'whole city' boiled up against St Paul (Acts 21:30), the mob dragged him away from the asylum which the temple offered, and beat him up (Acts 21:31), the Roman officer in charge tried to quell the riot and had him arrested and handcuffed (Acts 21:31, 32) and then inquired from the crowd about the charge against him (Acts 21:33); the crowd made no reasonable charge against him, but only became more incensed (Acts 21:34–36), because their victim was snatched from them and brought to the fort Antonia.

On the steps of the barracks St Paul managed to speak to the Roman officer, who so far had taken no steps to identify his prisoner (Acts 21:37). In fact it appears that he had gone after somebody else, an Egyptian trouble-maker (Acts 21:39). St Paul made himself known as an educated man who could speak Greek, and received permission to address the crowd. Apparently the Roman officer did not want to write any unnecessary reports, or to have an unsought for prisoner on his hands. He would have been well satisfied, if he could have let St Paul go, and he apparently saw a chance here enabling him to do so. All this is so natural that it is indeed surprising to see how many commentators have regarded this report as an attempt on the part of St Luke to curry favour with Rome.

We are surprised, however, to learn that St Paul addressed this Jewish mob which had attacked him with a most candid and moving speech, and we are inclined to ascribe this speech (Acts 22:1–21) to St Luke's own invention. He made St Paul give to the people to whom he belonged— and yet did not belong any longer—an elaborate account of his life. This was listened to as long as it recounted his Jewish antecedents, and even his conversion at Damascus. Only when he came to the crucial point of his mission to the Gentiles was he shouted down. In order to assess the accuracy of this speech we have to ask whether it conflicts with that account which we have from St Paul's own hand in Gal. 1–2. It is true to say that certain events reported here are not mentioned there. We have in Galatians no detailed description of St Paul's first sojourn at Jerusalem. On the other hand, the speech does not mention his preaching at Damascus or his journey to Arabia. However, it also suppresses the plot of the Hellenists against him, recorded in Acts 9:30, but relates his vision in the temple (Acts 22:17–21). All in all, accepting the paragraph division made by Moffatt before 22:17, we cannot find a contradiction in the actual facts mentioned. There is a great difference of approach, Galatians showing the heat of battle, Acts the coolness of contemplation; but the facts referred to do not seem irreconcilable. Acts 22:1–21 does not prove, as has been claimed, that St Paul was personally unknown to the author of Acts.

The reaction of the Jews has to be explained by the historical situation in which St Paul's arrest took place. In the years between A.D. 56–66 the intensity of Jewish hatred for all things foreign was white-hot. The description of their rage (Acts 22:22, 23) is thus only too credible. So also is the treatment of St Paul by the Roman soldiery (Acts 22:24) and the claim made by St Paul (Acts 22:25) that he was a Roman citizen. Internal evidence is therefore all in favour of the interview between St Paul and the Roman commanding officer (Acts 22:26–29). However, the question remains why St Luke reported all this at length. To draw an analogy between the sufferings of Jesus Christ and his martyrs became a stylistic principle in the Acts, to be continued in the whole literature dealing with Christian martyrs; but this principle does not explain the length or conciseness given to any such report. We assume, therefore, that it was St Luke's intention here to criticize the Roman system. We have to remember that St Luke was probably not a Roman citizen, but that Theophilus, to whom he dedicated his work, was a Roman of high standing, and that St Luke may have felt a strong impulse to draw his attention to the things which were going on in the Roman administration. Beyond that there was the general purpose of comparing the *pax Romana* with the peace of God within the kingdom of God. We must never forget that the angel's song near Bethlehem was a political pronouncement of very great vigour which rivalled the policy of imperial peace. When we see that every Pauline letter begins with words like 'Grace be to you and peace from God the Father and our Lord Jesus Christ', we feel that St Luke was here pleading for the Jerusalem Jews, who under this Roman despotism could not help reacting as unreasonably as they did. How could they be expected to welcome the Gentiles into the kingdom of heaven, if their earthly rule was like this? They were blinded against the rule of the only King who would never use violence, because they had nothing in their own experience to prepare them for such a possibility.

The Roman officer treated St Paul's case as a routine matter. It belonged to the jurisdiction of the local authority, the Jewish Sanhedrin, and before that court St Paul was arraigned (Acts 22:30).

The proceedings there are, we believe, consciously described by St Luke in the worst possible light. The Sanhedrin and in particular the high priest, we are given to understand, were unable to administer justice. As soon as St Paul began to speak, he was hit in the face at the order of the high priest (Acts 23:2). That made the apostle see red, and he cursed the high priest (23:3). Although he was made to apologize (23:4, 5), all his resentment against the corrupt Jewish hierarchy of his day was aroused, which as a Pharisee he had imbibed from his youth, and so he made his famous declaration (Acts 23:6):

I am a Pharisee, brothers, the son of Pharisees! it is for the hope of the resurrection from the dead that I am on trial!

Nobody, we believe, will quarrel with the second half of this statement; but the first has been censured most severely. Does it deserve such censure? The contention is that it contains a deliberate deception. St Paul, it is held, was not a Pharisee, but a Christian; but the two were by no means incompatible in the Church at Jerusalem, as we learn from Acts 15:5. The second criticism is that St Paul deliberately threw the meeting into confusion. That indeed seems to be true; but we feel strongly that that was not his fault, but the result of years of mismanagement by the high priests, and an ill-conducted opposition by the Pharisees. This Judaism needed salvation through Jesus Christ just as much as the Roman overlords.

St Paul could not escape the talons of the Roman eagle; he was taken back to the barracks (Acts 23:10), much bruised. There, however, he was given the protection which he could claim as a Roman citizen, and as a prisoner according to Roman law. Such, we hear, was the will of God, for Jesus himself appeared to his apostle in a vision in his cell, strengthening him with the words, 'as you have testified to me (been my martyr) at Jerusalem, so you must testify (be my martyr) at Rome' (23:11). Let us repeat that it was by no means a pleasure to be a prisoner of a Roman army unit; and those who see St Luke as an admirer of Rome on account of this description of St Paul's treatment, might reasonably be asked to do a spell of protective custody even under modern conditions. However, it was safety of a sort. All the same, the Jewish authorities could still express their desire to put St Paul on trial; but as yet he had not even been formally charged. Their hot-heads suggested using this chance for murdering him, and felt no hesitation in informing the high priests and elders about their plan (Acts 23:12–15).

The plot was thwarted by the intervention of St Paul's nephew, of whom we do not even know whether he was a Christian, informing first his uncle about it (Acts 23:16) and afterwards, on his advice, the Roman officer in charge (23:17–21). The Roman officer then arranged for St Paul a strong escort to Caesarea (Acts 23:22–24) and addressed also a short report to the governor (23:25–30). It is not our business either to point out how well this story agrees with Roman administrative practice, or to inquire into the family affairs of St Paul, but to find out what it tells us about God. For St Luke has incorporated it into his account of the early history of the Church for the express reason that it should instruct us about God. He wants us to see that the actions of men, even of wicked men, have to serve God's own ends. If we left out of consideration the significance of Christ's appearing to St Paul (Acts 23:11), this story would be no more than just another barrack-room tale. However, if we put this vision of Christ in the centre of the events described, it illustrates the importance of everyday attention to duty for the achievement of God's plans to an extent of which we may never be informed.

It is from consideration of the great consequences involved that the routine honesty of that military tribune Claudius Lysias (Acts 23:26) really begins to shine. We feel the contrast between the treatment of Jesus by the irresolute and intimidated Pontius Pilate, and the precise application of established rules by this subaltern as a matter of metaphysical principle.

IV

The soldiers did as they were told. They smuggled out St Paul at night from Jerusalem, and 'brought him by night to Antipatris' (Acts 23:31). That was a long ride to the plain near the shore of the Mediterranean, where Herod the Great had built a castle and named it after his father Antipater. The distance from Jerusalem is about forty miles, and there St Paul would be safe. From there a detachment of horse took him to Caesarea, the residence of the governor. At a short interview with Felix the governor, St Paul was formally made a state-prisoner (Acts 23:35). Once more the report is more detailed than one would expect. That is certainly due to the fact that these events were known to St Luke himself more fully than the earlier ones which he described. Nevertheless, there is also a theological reason behind his reporting them. He meant to contrast the tumultuous way of Jewish justice with the quiet, mechanical working of Roman justice. We, citizens of a civilized country, may find the Roman system infinitely superior. There was little shouting, no murder-plots, no street-fighting, when Rome took over the decision in any one case. On the other hand, there was no personal engagement either in this administration of justice. It was mechanical, almost soulless. It seems true to say that St Luke himself did not express preference for either system, but allowed the facts to speak for themselves. Neither system produced justice with a capital 'J'.

It was typical for the difference between the two systems that even the Jewish authorities themselves did not plead their own case before the governor Felix, but entrusted it to a professional barrister, Tertullus. His speech is interesting both in the things which he said as well as in those which he omitted. First of all, he omitted to mention the 'decrees of Caesar' (Acts 17:7). By these decrees both parties, the Synagogue as well as the Church, had been expelled from Rome, so that they did not constitute a suitable argument to be used by either of them. Moreover, the Emperor Claudius had been murdered in the meantine, and the attitude of Nero, his successor, may yet have been in doubt. The speech further omitted any definite application on the part of the Jews; 'Examine him for yourself, and you will be able to find out about all these charges of ours against him' (Acts 24:8). Thus Tertullus did not put an outright demand for the extradition of St Paul to the Jerusalem Sanhedrin, and it is indeed doubtful if any Roman authority would have consented to hand over a Roman citizen to any local authority.

Equally interesting is the actual tenor of the speech of Tertullus. First he put a most fulsome personal plea to this most corrupt of all the governors Rome ever sent to Judaea; and this is not only reported by St Luke in order to give the speech an authentic touch, but also to show how low these Jewish rulers would stoop to satisfy their animosity against St Paul. Once more the difference between the pretensions made by this Jewish hierarchy and its achievements is strongly but not unjustly emphasized. Secondly Tertullus characterized the Church at Jerusalem as 'the Nazarene sect' (Acts 24:5). This description is so interesting because we know that not only in Syria and in the Near East the Christians are known to this day as the Nazarenes, but that in the Talmud too, in the few places where it refers to Christians, these men are given the name of *Nozri*, the men from Nazareth. It appears, therefore, that just as Antioch gave to the Church the nickname of 'Christians', Jerusalem gave it the name of 'Nazarenes', which became as common in the East as 'Christians' in the West. 'Can anything good come out of Nazareth?' (John 1:46) is an apt commentary upon this development, for there seems to be no evidence to support the thesis of a Church Father of the fifth century, Epiphanius of Salamis in Cyprus, that there was a pre-Christian, Jewish sect of Nazarenes. We only mention it because it has given rise to all sorts of speculations amongst the more imaginative students of Christian origins.

St Paul's reply to this accusation was dignified and clear. The introductory remark addressed to Felix is intentionally kept short and, as far as etiquette allowed it, non-committal (Acts 24:10):

As I know you have administered justice in this nation for a number of years, . . .
I feel encouraged to make my defence.

This remark was indeed slightly ambiguous, in that Felix had no doubt been in charge of the administration of justice in the province of Judaea over a period of years; it left the question open, however, how he had discharged his duty. Actually Acts itself, as well as Jewish and pagan sources, agrees that he had done so most corruptly. However that may be, St Paul laid all the emphasis upon the long time which Felix had spent in Judaea. For this reason he should have been aware of the fact that St Paul had not lived in Jerusalem during all those years in which Felix had been in charge of the province (Acts 24:11). Consequently all that the Jewish authorities could plead of their own knowledge, and not from hearsay, was that he had caused the particular riot in the temple during which he had been arrested, and this St Paul denied vigorously (Acts 24:12, 13). He admitted his membership in the 'sect' of the Nazarenes, but he claimed to be a Jew (Acts 24:14–16). That means to say that for himself St Paul claimed that particular privilege of the Jews that the Romans should be impartial in matters of Jewish orthodoxy. The situation in which he found himself was an equivocal one. He was a Jew and he was a Roman. Unless he wanted to commit suicide, he had to make known his Roman citizenship to the Roman officer in charge at Jerusalem. Now, at his hearing before the governor Felix at Caesarea, he found it difficult to give an explanation for his expectation of the second coming of Jesus Christ in the near future in a way which would lay open the differences between his doctrine and the views of the Pharisaic party, which also believed in the 'resurrection from the dead'—not in some distant future, but as a living reality. He also had committed himself by his remark before the Sanhedrin. Thus the whole situation was so confused that almost anything that St Paul could say in his defence, was in danger of ringing oddly, or hollow, or even false in the ears of future generations.

What he actually said was yet simple enough. We have made an attempt at a more literal translation than that which is offered by Moffatt of Acts 24:17–21:

For several years, however, I spent my time in the preparation of gifts and contributions to my nation; and in discharging this task, whilst I was fulfilling a vow in the temple, far from any noisy crowd, certain Jews from Asia spotted me. These men should come forward and disclose the charge on which they would indict me. Or else, let the men here present state the crime of which they found me guilty when I stood before the Sanhedrin. Was it that one sentence, which I shouted: 'It is for the resurrection of the dead that I stand here today to be judged'?

Even Felix, who knew about 'the Way', i.e. the Church (Acts 24:22), could not fail to detect the weakness of the argument propounded by Tertullus in favour of the Jewish Sanhedrin. However, there was only a semblance of that military precision, which his subaltern at Jerusalem had shown, when he made his decision to remand St Paul and to hear in full the evidence which that officer might be able to give. Apparently he never carried out this decision either. However, the Jews could be satisfied that he kept St Paul in custody, even if it was honourable custody. Occasionally he produced him as an entertainment for his wife, Drusilla, a princess of the Herodian house. He listened to his sermons, but became uneasy when the apostle began to expound the doctrine of the Last Judgment. He held him to ransom, but the Church at Jerusalem never offered any price for the apostle; and in the meantime he conversed with him. Once more we have to remember the loneliness and the boredom of these Roman courtiers abroad, to appreciate the historical situation; but we should not overlook the lesson that loneliness and boredom do not condition a man to the willing acceptance of the gospel. St Paul may have succeeded in awakening his conscience, but he failed to convert him. For in the end he left St Paul behind in custody, to ingratiate himself with his enemies, the Jews, when he was recalled to Rome to stand his trial. The Jews had accused him because of riots at Caesarea, which he had cruelly suppressed. Needless to say, his court connections saw him safely through his ordeal.

10 St Paul and the Power of Rome

I

The man who followed Felix was the one honourable governor Rome ever sent to Judaea. Jews and Romans are both agreed on this point. Porcius Festus was dry, even dour; he had been a soldier all his life. However, he had a sense of honour and fair play which was in the best Roman tradition. He was determined to see justice done, even to a Roman citizen like St Paul, if he had broken the Jewish law; but it would be real justice. Thus, although he was only a few days in the province, he was not prepared to hand St Paul to the Jewish authorities without having examined his case properly himself. Although this year A.D. 60 was a year of increasing tension, he met the representations made to him by the Jewish authorities with a courteous firmness (Acts 25:4 f.):

> Festus replied that Paul would be kept in custody at Caesarea, but that he himself meant to leave for Caesarea before long—'when', he added, 'your competent authorities can come along with me and charge the man with whatever crime he has committed'.

Thus the Jewish authorities had got no further with Festus than they had with Felix, and they had to try the legal way once more.

It is surprising to notice that the Jewish authorities, who had held their hand with Felix till he left, sprang into action as soon as Festus had arrived. This can only be explained by the strained relations between them and Felix, whom they eventually denounced at the imperial court. That made it an obvious impossibility for them to offer him any bribe for the handing over of St Paul which, in different circumstances, he would probably have accepted. In addition there had been the murder-plot, which the centurion Lysias had foiled. It is significant that, as soon as the new governor had arrived, that plan was revived (Acts 25:3), but that it was left dormant as long as Felix was in office. Admittedly, Caesarea was not a place where such an attempt was likely to succeed with impunity. However, it appears to us that Felix had given St Paul that special protection which the sustained interest of the governor in the person of his prisoner was likely to provide. Thus, in view of the fact that Acts mentions his venality, and by no means makes a hero of him, we feel inclined to take this second murder-plot seriously, and not just as a rumour. It must not be forgotten, how heinously the Jewish high priest only two years later disposed of James of Jerusalem during the interregnum after the death of Festus.

The tenor of the report about St Paul's second trial differs considerably from that of the first. Felix, we were given to understand, had known sufficiently well about what was going on between the Jewish Sanhedrin and the 'Nazarenes', and it would have been his plain duty to release St Paul. In the trial itself, however, he had insisted upon formal propriety being observed. Festus, on the other hand, was new to the job and had no inside information. Thus the proceedings got out of hand. According to Acts 25:7, there was little formality, let alone dignity, in them; and St Paul was thus denied the protection every prisoner at the bar derives from the observation of legal minutiae. Numbers of charges were brought against him by the implacable Jewish chief priests, and the scene reminds us of Jesus's trial before Pilate (Mark 15:3 f.):

> Then the high priest brought many accusations against him, and once more Pilate asked him, 'Have you no reply to make? Look at all their charges against you'.

This technique of covering an adversary with as many charges as may be reasonably invented, because one or the other may yet appear to demand a closer investigation is, unfortunately, not uncommon in some forms of polemic to this day, Like so many other judges, Festus was impressed by this hostile approach of the Jewish authorities to St Paul. The apostle had no other defence than a straight denial of all the charges (Acts 25:8). However, this defence was worthless where the judge was as ignorant of the actual conditions as Festus. It was also particularly dangerous for St Paul, since Festus was unsuspecting too of the pressure which the Jews would be able to bring to bear upon him if he sat in judgment at Jerusalem. He seems to have been quite unaware of Pilate's experience at the trial of Jesus, and to have had only that one ambition, to show fairness to the Jews.

Thus the alternative for St Paul lay exclusively between Jerusalem and Rome. As a Roman citizen he had the right to appeal to the Emperor, to have his case tried before a Roman court, and in desperation he made up his mind to use this right (Acts 25:10 f.):

> I have done no wrong whatever to the Jews—you know that perfectly well. If I am a criminal, if I have done anything that deserves death, I do not object to die; but if there is nothing in any of their charges against me, then no one can give me up to them. I appeal to Caesar!

The governor then consulted with his legal advisers, and entered his verdict (Acts 25:12):

You have appealed to Caesar? Very well, you must go to Caesar!

Such was the Roman administration that the affairs of Roman citizens were centralized at Rome, even though under Felix's predecessor a Roman centurion of the name of Celer had actually been executed at Jerusalem, to satisfy the Jews who had been outraged by him. The Emperor was the successor of the people's tribunes of old. He had the duty of protecting Roman citizens abroad as well as in the capital; and if there was a reason for prosecuting them, he had them committed before the ordinary courts at Rome. The vision of St Paul (Acts 23:11) when Jesus had assured him that he would be his witness in Rome, was to come true by the simplest and most common means, and that is the message and the comfort of this passage: all the adverse circumstances, all the heartsearchings of St Paul, and all the bungling of the Roman authorities did not alter God's plan one whit.

However, these circumstances caused much trouble to the governor Festus, for he had to write a report to the Emperor. Being an honest man, he wanted to state the case as clearly and faithfully as he could, and for this purpose he used the opportunity which was offered him at his first meeting with Herod Agrippa II, the brother-in-law of Felix (Acts 25:13 ff.). It was an extraordinary step which Festus took when consulting the king about the case of St Paul. Agrippa II, it is true, was a Roman citizen of high standing, and a friend and ally of the Emperor; nevertheless, he was also a suzerain prince. Formally no objection could be made to his being consulted; from a political point of view, however, such a step could constitute a dangerous precedent. There is a marked difference between asking him for his opinion and inviting him, as Festus did, to take part in the proceedings.

What we would like to know is the basis for Festus's description of St Paul's case to him in Acts 25:14-21. We suspect that St Luke shows himself exceptionally well informed. To judge the passage, we should compare it with a report concerning a prisoner who was being sent to Rome half a century later by Pliny the Younger, governor of Bithynia. This is found in his correspondence with the Emperor Trajan (*Epistles* x:74):

Your Majesty, the soldier Appuleius of the garrison at Nicomedia has reported to me a certain Callidromus who, when detained by the bakers Maximus and Dionysius as their employee, had taken refuge at your statue, and had stated that he had originally been a slave of one Laberius Maximus, had then been captured in Moesia by Susagus and subsequently been presented to Pacorus, the king of Parthia, whom he had served for several years. From him he claims to have fled and to have made his way to Nicomedia. When he was brought before me, I decided on his story to have him sent to you.

Allowing for the differences caused by the different status of this unfortunate Callidromus, we have yet in this letter a comparable original report about an interesting prisoner, who was sent to the Emperor. In tenor this report is so similar to that in Acts 25:14 ff., that we venture to conclude that St Luke fashioned this speech of Festus upon the official report to the Emperor, to which he probably had access on the journey to Rome. For, of course, he could have no knowledge of what had happened at the interview betweeen Festus and Agrippa. He was, however, like many other historians of his time—Josephus for instance— a glutton for documentary evidence, and knew how to use it to the best advantage in his history.

II

There followed then the famous appearance of St Paul before King Agrippa II, the last of the Herodians, and the Roman Festus. Its introduction shows clearly how reluctant St Luke was to invent anything. For it is evident that Acts 25:24–28 does not contain anything that has not been said already in verses 14–21. It only serves to give its proper place to the candid admission of Festus in 25:26, 'I have nothing definite to write to the Sovereign about him.'

It is for this reason that we are reluctant to accept Cadbury's suggestion[1] that it was a kind of snobbery on the part of St Luke when he reported (Acts 25:23):

So next day Agrippa and Bernice proceeded with great pomp to the hall of audience, accompanied by the military commanders and the prominent civilians of the town.

Cadbury himself does not deny that the assembly did in fact consist of the groups here mentioned; and it is certain that a state visit like the one of Agrippa II at Caesarea would demand such an audience. Neither is it at all improbable that a gala performance of Roman justice should have been staged in honour of such a visitor by the governor Festus. After all, it was

[1] H. J. Cadbury, *The Book of Acts in History* (New York, 1955), p. 43.

the solemn duty of the representative of Rome in the province to establish the *pax Romana* by his administration of law and justice. The incident as such is, therefore, well authenticated by external as well as by internal evidence, even if the choice of the case made by Festus may appear somewhat unwise.

We have to ask, however, what the reason was which made St Luke report this incident at length, if we reject Cadbury's suggestion, as we feel we must. For if Cadbury were right in assuming that St Luke was out to make an impression upon Theophilus and other readers by the earthly importance of St Paul and the Christian Church already at the time before the fall of Jerusalem, Acts 25:23 would be in need of a considerable enlargement. As it stands, it is out of proportion to St Paul's following speech (Acts 26:2–23), one of the longest and most elaborate speeches in Acts. If, however, this speech is to be regarded as the chief substance of the whole passage, as is obviously the case, the whole event must be judged in a different light. It is clearly meant as an illustration of Jesus's saying in Luke 21:12 ff.:

you will be dragged before kings and governors for the sake of my name. That will turn out an opportunity for you to bear witness. So resolve to yourselves that you will not rehearse your defence beforehand, for I will give you words and wisdom that not one of your opponents will be able to meet or refute.

Once St Paul's sermon before Agrippa and Festus is seen in this light, there also appears a sufficient reason for its being more or less a repetition of that in Acts 22:1–21. For the first half of Luke 21:12 reads:

But before all that, men will lay hands on you and persecute you, handing you over to synagogues and prisons.

St Luke, therefore, wanted to make it quite clear that for the apostle the raging Jerusalem mob and the brilliant assembly at Caesarea were no more than two aspects of the same picture; and that—to our way of thinking—can hardly be represented as a piece of snobbery on his part.

Once more we have to refrain from discussing St Paul's sermon. We cannot even dwell upon the differences between the description of his conversion at Damascus here and that in the earlier accounts. They centre, as you may know, round Acts 22:9, 'My companions saw the light, but they did not hear the voice of him who talked to me', when compared with 26:13 f. and 9:3. We have to deal, however, with the reactions of St Paul's audience: Festus's reply (Acts 26:24), 'Paul, you are quite mad! Your great learning is driving you insane!' and King Agrippa's remark

I

(Acts 26:28), 'At this rate . . . it won't be long before you believe you have made a Christian of me!' For these two replies echo St Paul's own summing-up remark in I Cor. 1:23:

our message is Christ the crucified—a stumbling-block to Jews, 'sheer folly' to Gentiles.

The analogy is so close that we refuse to take it as accidental. It is, of course, not impossible to assume that these remarks were actually made by Festus and Agrippa. However, there is not a very great likelihood that this should be so. How, we would ask, was Festus to know about the 'great learning' of St Paul? The speech itself shows little of it. St Paul, it is true, mentions his early career as a Pharisee (Acts 26:5), but he does not mention his studies 'at the feet of Gamaliel' (Acts 22:3); and the chief content of his speech is his vision at Damascus. In fact, although St Paul maintained (Acts 26:22),

To this day I have had the help of God in standing, as I now do, to testify alike to low and high, never uttering a single syllable beyond what the prophets and Moses predicted was to take place,

the speech shows none of St Paul's erudition as an Old Testament scholar, comparable to (e.g.) Gal. 4:21 ff. Therefore, even if Festus had perused the documents in St Paul's case, this speech was in no way the kind of speech which could have emphasized St Paul's learning.

The only reason one might feel inclined to admit that the governor should have passed a polite remark about the speaker's learning, is the rhetorical attitude of St Paul, recorded in Acts 26:1: 'at this Paul stretched out his hand and began his defence'. Now it was quite customary to congratulate a professional rhetor on his great learning; but the argument for the historicity of Festus's rather left-handed compliment founded upon this remains weak nevertheless. After all, St Paul did not make a professional speech, but conducted his defence at his trial. Agrippa's remark, moreover, does not have any support whatsoever. St Luke, we feel sure, inserted both replies in order to show that the gospel of Christ was not addressed to an audience like this; but that the two were nevertheless carrying out the will of Jesus Christ.

When they had retired, Festus and Agrippa agreed that there had been a miscarriage of justice: 'this man has done nothing to deserve death or imprisonment' (Acts 26:31). Have we not heard similar words spoken in a similar context? 'This man has done no harm' (Luke 23:41) was what the one crucified robber said to the other at Jesus's passion. Is that to be regarded as a mere coincidence? If not, how far are we entitled to stretch the analogy? We would not advise any comparison between Festus and Agrippa on the one hand and the two robbers on the other. We would, however, take seriously the atmosphere of Christ's passion which is suggested not only in this, but also by the analogy to Pilate's question (Luke 23:22): 'But what crime has he committed? I have found nothing about him that deserves death; so I shall release him with a whipping.' For these words make a fitting background to Agrippa's final statement (Acts 26:32):

'He might have been released', said Agrippa to Festus, 'if he had not appealed to Caesar'.

When interpreting Acts 26:30–32, it is impossible to forget the stark fact that the Emperor to whom St Paul had been driven by circumstances to appeal was Nero. Nero's name, however, was to be discredited by his cruel persecution of the Christians at Rome in A.D. 64. Once more it is impossible for the honest historian to make a definite statement as to whether this event caused St Luke to make use of these allusions to Christ's passion. For the only contemporary source describing the Neronian persecution comes from the pen of the pagan historian, Tacitus. However, the question must be asked whether it seems improbable that St Luke should have had this persecution in mind, when he formulated this discussion between Festus and Agrippa. He cannot have known anything about the actual words exchanged between the two after retiring from the hall of judgment. We therefore suggest that these allusions to Christ's passion constitute a hint given us as to St Paul's ultimate fate.

III

Thus St Paul's journey to Rome is given by St Luke something of the inevitability of an ancient tragedy. It starts tamely enough. Two of his companions on his last journey are specially mentioned. The one is the Roman officer in charge of him, Julius, a centurion of the Augustan cohort. We are surprised, however, at the other, 'a Macedonian from Thessalonica called Aristarchus' (Acts 27:2). For we remember that this name has already appeared on the list of St Paul's companions on his last journey to Jerusalem (Acts 20:4), and we know from Col. 1:1 and 4:7, that Timothy and Tychicus, who both appear on this list also, were with him during his imprisonment in Rome. We would not have been able to account satisfactorily for this curious singling out of Aristarchus, were it not for Col. 4:10, 'Aristarchus my fellow-prisoner salutes you.' Of the reasons for the imprisonment of Aristarchus St Luke has told us nothing; and if St Paul's Epistle to the Colossians had not survived, the two verses in which his name is mentioned in Acts might have given rise to all sorts of conjectures.

The first stage of the journey too is filled only with mental strain. It took St Paul for the last time along the coasts where he had spread the gospel of Christ. He was allowed by the Roman officer to pay a visit to the Christian Church at Sidon (Acts 27:3). He saw from afar once more the hills of Cyprus (27:4) and from there the ship took him all along the shores of Cilicia, his native province, and of Pamphylia, where his great adventure of converting the Gentiles had begun (27:5). This last rehearsal of his past life came to an end when, at Myra in Lycia, he and his companions had to change ship (27:6). It is followed by the tumultuous events of the famous voyage to Crete, and the shipwreck on the shore of the island of Malta.

This whole story is told us in order to show the way in which St Paul's authority revealed itself amongst his fellow-travellers. If St Luke had set out with the intention of writing a life of St Paul, he would not have omitted the many incidents enumerated in II Cor. 11:23 ff. We learn from that account of his sufferings for the sake of Christ, which comes from the apostle's own pen, that he had been shipwrecked already three times before he embarked upon this his last journey (II Cor. 11:25), and St Luke has not so much as mentioned this. Admittedly, he may not have been present at any of these disasters; but it seems highly improbable that he possessed no information about them. It was his free decision that he would report only this one catastrophe on St Paul's last journey. Having realized this, we can only assume that he did so, because this journey was to lead St Paul to his last and most important assignment, his martyrdom at Rome.

Once this purpose of St Luke's report is fully understood, the progress of the story which he tells us becomes clearly evident. At the beginning of the journey, travelling from Myra to Fair Havens in Crete (Acts 27:6–8), we see St Paul as the mere object of Roman administration, a prisoner in chains, aboard ship to be transported to Italy together with other, seemingly more important, passengers and goods, entrusted to a crew from Alexandria, the biggest port of the Empire. At Fair Havens St Paul suddenly emerges as a man of experience and common sense, suggesting reasonable precautions which should be taken by the captain and his crew (Acts 27:9, 10) but because he was only a prisoner, and not even a professional sailor, his advice was turned down by his gaoler, the Roman officer in charge of him, who accepted the sailors' plan of sailing to a more suitable harbour for the ship to pass the inclement season (Acts 27:11, 12). That plan, we are told, miscarried completely, because a gale sprang up which at this time of the year blew with such regularity that it had even received the nickname of Euraquilo,[1] the 'Nor' easter' (Acts 27:13–16). Under this emergency every device which the seamen's craft had thought of was employed, first to save the ship and its cargo, and eventually to save the naked lives of those aboard ship (Acts 27:16–19), until in the end all hope was abandoned (Acts 27:20). At this point St Paul arose for the second time, making himself known as the man whom God had chosen to act as the messenger from the eternal King, Jesus Christ, to the earthly Emperor (Acts 27:21–26). At last it is revealed that everything—cargo, ship, crew and Roman officer—has been sent on this journey only in order to serve God's purpose with his apostle. However, in his mercy, God has made a gift of the lives of all the people aboard ship to his apostle.

It cannot be doubted that the miracle of Jonah was in St Luke's mind when he described this scene; nevertheless, he has made little use of it. Jonah saved his companions by sacrificing his own life; St Paul did the same by imposing his moral and intellectual superiority upon the Roman officer in charge (Acts 27:31). This man, having trusted the sailors once too often, now relied upon St Paul's judgment and prevented the sailors from leaving the ship (27:32). There followed St Paul's advice that all the ship's company should eat; 'Take some food then, I beg of you; it will keep you alive. You are going to be saved! Not a hair of your heads will perish' (Acts 27:34). These words may mean very little by themselves; however, the following verse, which is in itself very mysterious, may fill St Paul's exhortation with an unexpected meaning (Acts 27:35):

With these words he took a loaf, and after thanking God, in presence of them all, broke it and began to eat.

No instructed Christian reader can fail to overhear the parallel existing with I Cor. 11:23 f., 'the Lord Jesus Christ took a loaf, and after thanking God he broke it, saying, "This means my body broken for you; do this in memory of me".' Are we then to understand that St Paul here celebrated the Eucharist on behalf of an unsuspecting, pagan company? It

---

[1] Moffatt retains the inferior form 'Euroclydon'.

seems that we can hardly escape this conclusion, although the consequences of drawing it are very serious. The reason why it seems necessary to come to such a conclusion is that Acts 20:7, 11, contains the technical description of the Eucharist as 'the breaking of bread', and the same passage makes it clear that it was a special service, and that St Luke did not regard every meal as sacramental, as the Quakers do.

We, therefore, assume that St Paul at this juncture celebrated the Eucharist on behalf of the whole ship's company, although he did not communicate it to them. For 'then they all cheered up and took food for themselves' (Acts 27:36). We also feel that this exegesis gives the necessary background for the soldiers' plan (Acts 27:42 f.) to kill all the prisoners, as well as for the officer's preventing its execution. Whilst St Paul had saved their lives by performing a sacramental act on their behalf, these soldiers had still no other idea in their minds than to kill. It is very likely that they would have been taken to the strictest account for any missing prisoner, and that proof of his death would have been their surest safeguard; but it must not be overlooked either that it was probably St Luke's intention to stress that St Paul's action did not secure eternal salvation for them. It did, however, secure their earthly survival.

A phrase from Kipling's *Kim* may be helpful to clear up the next scene on the island of Malta where the shipwrecked people had come ashore (Acts 28:1)—the phrase, 'I will be your sacrifice'. In that setting this is a very pagan idea, but it is also the basis of our Christian faith, Jesus Christ being our sacrifice, atoning for our sins. All over the world there lingers a suspicion that evil deeds must be avenged, and in the time of St Paul a special goddess was entrusted with such vengeance which could not be wrought by human agency. The name of this goddess was Dike, 'Justice'. St Paul, having established himself as the messenger of God amongst his companions, was yet to the islanders no more than one of those who had escaped from the sea. However, Jesus had assured his disciples (Luke 10:19):

I have indeed given you the power of treading on serpents.

This was also an established, old sign of divine protection and grace. In the passage from the Third Gospel it has to be regarded as a quotation from Ps. 91:13,

you can walk over reptiles and cobras, trampling on lions and on dragons,

but pagan parallels are not wanting either, and these are of importance here. For when St Paul was bitten by a viper immediately after he had escaped the terror of the deep, it was for the islanders who beheld it a test-case of divine justice (Acts 28:4):

This man must be a murderer! He has escaped the sea, but Justice will not let him live.

However, when it appeared that St Paul was miraculously preserved, the natives 'changed their minds and held he was a god' (Acts 28:6). How can we explain that St Paul did nothing to undeceive them? Had he forgotten his experiences at Lystra (Acts 14:14 ff.) or had he changed his mind since that time? We believe that neither of these two answers would serve as a sufficient explanation of this passage; it is rather to be assumed that already St Luke held the view, which became generally accepted within the Church in the following century, that the martyrs were made Christ-like; and he wants us to understand that St Paul was on his way to martyrdom. Acccordingly St Paul's powers of healing came also strongly to the fore (Acts 28:7–10).

Nothing could from now on deflect St Paul from his way to martyrdom. A ship was ready at the island of Malta to receive him and his companions (Acts 28:11); the voyage from the island to Puteoli was uneventful (28:12–13) and when he arrived there, he found fellow-Christians to receive him (28:14). The Roman Christians had even walked out of the city to receive him on his way there; 'and when Paul saw them he thanked God and took courage' (Acts 28:15). This is, for the last time, once more an enigmatic remark of St Luke's. We can only enumerate some possible reasons for St Paul's encouragement at his reception at Rome. We would rule out the suggestion that he was simply worried about his coming trial, and that the Roman Christians reassured him on the chances that his case would be dismissed by the court. For the word chosen by St Luke for 'took courage' is not only the same as in John 16:33, 'but courage! I have conquered the world'; it refers directly to Paul's vision at Jerusalem (Acts 23:11), 'Courage! as you have testified to me at Jerusalem, so you must testify at Rome,' and this parallel is intentional and should be kept in mind. More probability may be attached to the explanation that St Paul was encouraged with regard to the relationship between his churches and the Church at Rome, which was, as we have seen, not of his foundation. The fact that he was well received by the Roman Christians not only reassured him on this point, but it also finally established that the Churches of the East and the West were one, extending from Jerusalem to Rome. Nevertheless, this recognition should be enlarged upon, for the coming martyrdom must not be forgotten. For it is indeed questionable whether there can be any martyrdom without a Church. If the Church at Rome had disowned him, would St Paul have been a martyr? One more thought comes to mind. Some at least of these Christians would have to undergo martyrdom too in the Neronian persecution. May it not be that St Paul was also encouraged when seeing them welcoming him, the martyr of Christ, by the assurance that they also would be able to stand?

There remained yet one matter for St Paul to attend to, his relation to the Jews; and as he was given a certain amount of freedom (Acts 28:16), he invited the leaders of Roman Jewry to meet him. The days of 'the decrees of Caesar' (Acts 17:7) were long past. These leaders of the Jews were friendly disposed towards St Paul as a person, and assured him that they had not received any adverse information regarding him from Jerusalem; 'but as regards this sect, we are well aware that objections are taken to it on all hands' (Acts 28:22). Thus St Paul took the last opportunity that was offered to him at Rome of preaching the gospel of Christ to the Jews. However, even now his pleading was in vain. Jesus himself had told his disciples (Luke 8:10):

It is granted you to understand the open secrets of the Reign of God, but the others get it in parables, so that
for all their seeing they may not see,
and for all their hearing they may not understand.

St Paul all through his ministry up to this last attempt had to undergo the very same experience, and St Luke wanted to emphasize this point when he made the apostle quote the same prophecy from Isa. 6:9 f. (Acts 28:26 f.). The work of Saul, the Jew and Pharisee, who had been called by Christ to preach the gospel 'to the Jews first, and to the Gentiles also' (Rom. 1:16), was thus accomplished. And St Paul 'for two full years . . . remained in his private lodging, welcoming anyone who came to visit him; he preached the Reign of God and taught about the Lord Jesus Christ quite openly and unmolested' (Acts 28:30, 31).

It seems unthinkable that there should have been any continuation of St Luke's account of the travels of St Paul, for after those two years came the year 64, the year of the Neronian persecution and of St Paul's martyrdom. It may, however, be asked whether St Luke should not have given an account of this? The answer is that it would have been impossible for St Luke to distinguish between the death of the apostle and of the hundreds who were martyred along with him. For all their sufferings were one and their witness to Christ was also one. We have already seen, how

St Luke found it difficult to keep out the martyrdom of Aristarchus, St Paul's fellow-prisoner, from his history. He could not bring himself to suppress his name, although he failed to mention his sufferings and his supreme sacrifice. Therefore, St Paul would either have lost his individuality in a description of the general suffering of the Church at Rome, and that would have spoilt the purpose of St Luke's report, or else his martyrdom would have had to be given a special emphasis, and that would have brought it dangerously near to the passion of Jesus Christ himself. Neither way was therefore practicable for St Luke or, indeed, for the Church. For upon earth St Paul was undoubtedly a special case, as the apostle of Jesus Christ to the Gentiles; before God, however, he was himself no more than any other member of Christ's body, the Church. No more and no less—for all Christ's martyrs, whatever their earthly achievements, are one in him. Finally, it must not be forgotten that St Luke, being a disciple of St Paul and expecting, like him, the early Second Coming of the Lord, would consider the earthly death of his teacher far less important than later generations of Christians were to do.

This, at last, brings us to the formula which might be used for a title of the book of the New Testament, which we have tried to study in detail in these lectures. We would characterize it as:

The Gospel of the Holy Spirit in the Church Militant Here in Earth.

Bibliography

Barrett, C. K., *Luke the Historian in Recent Study* (London, 1961).

Bell, H. I., *Jews and Christians in Egypt* (London, 1924).

Blass, F., *Acta Apostolorum sive Lucas ad Theophilum liber alter* (Göttingen, 1895).

Blass, F., *Acta Apostolorum secundum formam quae videtur Romanam* (Leipzig, 1896).

Brandon, S. G. F., *The Fall of Jerusalem and the Christian Church* (London, 1951).

Bruce, F. F., *The Acts of the Apostles* (London, 1952).

Cadbury, H. J., 'Some Semitic personal names in Luke–Acts', in *Amicitiae Corolla*, ed. H. G. Wood (London, 1933).

Cadbury, H. J., *The Book of Acts in History* (New York, 1955).

Caird, G. B., *The Apostolic Age* (London, 1955).

Dalman, G. H., *Arbeit und Sitte in Palästina* I–VI (Gütersloh, 1928–39).

Ehrhardt, A., *The Framework of the New Testament Stories* (Manchester, 1964).

Erbt, W., *Von Jerusalem nach Rom* (Berlin, 1896).

Fink, R. O., Hoey, A. S., Snyder, W. F., 'The *Feriale Duranum*', *Yale Classical Studies* 7 (1940).

Foakes-Jackson, F. J., *The Acts of the Apostles* (London, 1931).

Harnack, A., *The Acts of the Apostles*, E. T. (London, 1909).

Iames, M. R., *Apocrypha Anecdota* I, II = *Texts and studies* ii, 3; v, 1 (Cambridge, 1893–7).

James, M. R., *The Apocryphal New Testament* (Oxford, 1924).

Leon, H. J., *The Jews of Ancient Rome* (Philadelphia, 1960).

Lightfoot, J. B., *Saint Paul's Epistle to the Galatians* (London, 1865).

Loisy, A., *The Origins of the New Testament*, E. T. (London, 1950).

Loisy, A., *Les Actes des Apôtres* (Paris, 1920).

Meyer, E., *Ursprung und Anfänge des Christentums* I, III (Berlin, 1921, 1923).

Rieger, P., and Vogelstein, H., *Geschichte der Juden in Rom* (Berlin, 1896).

Ramsay, W. M., *Historical Commentary on St Paul's Epistle to the Galatians* (London, 1899).

Ramsay, W. M., *St. Paul the Traveller and the Roman Citizen* (London, 1895).

Simon, M., *Verus Israel* (Paris, 1948).

Wette, W. M. L. de, *Kurze Erklärung der Apostelgeschichte* [4], ed. F. Overbeck (Leipzig, 1927).

Zahn, T., *Die Apostelgeschichte des Lucas* [4] (Leipzig, 1927).

Index

I. Subjects

Index to subjects

Silas 91, 96 f.
Simeon 50 f.
Simon Magus 42 ff.
Social conditions 20, 22, 29, 95
Sources (Luke's) 1, 3, 4, 17 ff., 25,
  27 f., 32, 34, 36 ff., 44, 59, 61, 90, 98,
  101, 104, 109 f., 114, 120
Spain 3
Stephen 3, 26 ff., 40 f., 44, 58, 67, 109
Stoning 32 ff., 84
Style 1, 4, 5, 15, 18, 35, 45, 55, 108
Synagogue(s) 8, 20, 31, 33, 53, 73, 76,
  85, 90, 95 ff., 100, 102

Tacitus 12, 123
Ta'eb 41
Talmud 14, 30, 114
Tarsus 63 f., 70, 91
Tatian 7
Teachers 85
Temple 15 f., 19, 26, 31, 33 f., 44,
  50, 53, 109, 115
Temple of Diana 49
Temple at Leontopolis 33
Tertullian 10 f.
Theme (of Acts) 9, 11, 39 f., 60, 124

Theology 2, 7, 12, 14, 39, 102, 104,
  106 f., 113
Theophilus 1, 60, 111, 121
Thucydides 12
Timothy 37, 92, 97, 109, 123
Title (of Acts) 9, 12, 39, 129
Titus 72, 86, 92
Titus (Emperor) 76
Toleration 29, 76
Trade 49 f.
Tradition 7, 25, 102
Trajan 119
Twelve 12 ff., 37, 39 ff., 53, 59, 69
Typology 55, 60

Universalism 75 f.
Unity 71, 127

We-report 3, 93, 109

Young men 20

Zaqen 73
Zadokite document 20
Zealots 76
Zion 15 f

134

II. Biblical and other ancient references

Index to biblical references